THE
SUSTAINABLE
ENTERPRISE

Books are to be returned on or before
the last date below.

**7−DAY
LOAN**

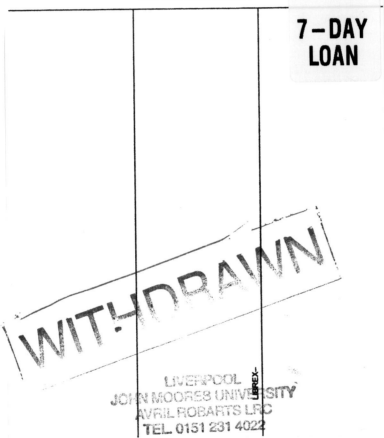

THE
SUSTAINABLE
ENTERPRISE

Profiting from best practice

2nd edition

Consultant editor:
Jonathan Reuvid

Simmons & Simmons

KOGAN PAGE

London and Philadelphia

Publisher's note

Every possible effort has been made to ensure that the information contained in this book is accurate at the time of going to press, and the publishers and authors cannot accept responsibility for any errors or omissions, however caused. No responsibility for loss or damage occasioned to any person acting, or refraining from action, as a result of the material in this publication can be accepted by the editor, the publisher or any of the authors.

First published in Great Britain and the United States in 2005 by Kogan Page Limited
Second edition 2006

120 Pentonville Road
London N1 9JN
United Kingdom
www.kogan-page.co.uk

525 South 4th Street, #241
Philadelphia PA 19147
USA

ISBN 0 7494 4643 9

British Library Cataloguing-in-Publication Data

A CIP record for this book is available from the British Library.

Library of Congress Cataloging-in-Publication Data

Sustainable enterprise : profiting from best practice / Jonathan Reuvid [editor].—2nd ed.
    p. cm.
  Includes bibliographical references and index.
    ISBN 0-7494-4643-9 (alk. paper)
  1. Social responsibility of business. 2. Business enterprises—Environmental aspects. 3. Small business—Environmental aspects. 4. Industrial management. 5. Factory and trade waste—Environmental aspects. 6. Pollution prevention. 7. Business ethics. I. Reuvid, Jonathan.
  HD60.S887 2006
  658.4'08—dc22

                                                                    2006023011

Typeset by JS Typesetting Ltd, Porthcawl, Mid Glamorgan
Printed and bound in Great Britain by Cambridge University Press

transport**energy** >
BestPractice

Free advice and information on travel planning

It is a fact that UK Business loses a staggering £20 billion a year through road congestion alone. To reduce such losses and improve efficiency and effectiveness, the Government's TransportEnergy BestPractice programme offers professional advice to help organisations adopt and implement their specific plan.

What is a travel plan?

A travel plan is a package of measures designed to reduce reliance on the car for commuter, business and leisure travel. By reducing the amount of car traffic associated with a site, a travel plan will help tackle the transport and traffic problems that affect all organisations.

What are the benefits of a travel plan

Developing a travel plan can deliver direct benefits to your organisation, your employees and the environment. These may include:

> Control of your transport and travel costs
> Manage your car parking problems effectively on and off site
> Address staff recruitment and retention problems
> Reduce congestion around your site
> Ensure site developments can proceed
> Improve your corporate image and public perception
> Have a site that is easily accessible to all of your staff, visitors and clients
> Reduced fuel costs and improved efficiency

Who are we?

TransportEnergy is a division of the Energy Saving Trust; a non-profit organisation established by the Government to help the UK meet its international commitments to reduce greenhouse gas emissions. Through its BestPractice programme, TransportEnergy provides authoritative, independent and free information and advice to assist with the development and implementation of travel plans.

What do we offer?
On-site expert advice

The TransportEnergy BestPractice programme offers up to five days of free site-specific advice from an independent travel expert to help organisations develop a travel plan. The site-specific advice scheme is fully funded and offers participants a high quality service. All workplaces based in England can benefit from the scheme, in particular private businesses, hospitals, local authorities, government agencies, tourist attractions and leisure sites.

Publications

Through this programme, TransportEnergy offers a wide range of publications including our quarterly newsletter 'Travel Plan News', good practice guides, case studies, training material and information leaflets on all aspects of travel planning.

Hotline and website

For more information on how we can help you, or to apply for site-specific advice, please visit our website at:
www.transportenergy.org.uk/travelplans
Alternatively, you can call the TransportEnergy Hotline on **0845 602 1425**.

Department for
Transport

TE173

Joined up thinking on purchasing and supply

In today's competitive arena, an effective purchasing and supply strategy can help you stay one step ahead, driving down costs whilst improving efficiencies from the ground up.

Purchasing - a key business process

When you consider that the value of bought-in goods can be up to 80% of turnover or revenue, the power of procurement can never be overstated. So it makes sense to lead from the front and work with your purchasing and supply team to improve performance. In fact, developing the right procurement strategy could be one of the best investments your organisation ever makes.

CIPS - become part of our network

As the leading authority on purchasing and supply, CIPS can help you stay informed on the issues that matter. By becoming an Affiliate Member of CIPS, you'll have access to the latest information and guidance on a whole range of purchasing and supply issues – helping you create a clear, effective purchasing strategy to move your business forward. To find out more visit www.cips.org or call 01780 756 777.

For further information
please contact:

tel: +44 (0)1780 756 777
fax: +44 (0)1780 751 610
email: info@cips.org
web: www.cips.org

THE
CHARTERED INSTITUTE OF
PURCHASING & SUPPLY

Contents

Contributors' notes

Tim Ashmore is an independent energy management consultant. Previously, he worked for a large utility supplier providing energy management services to its clients. Tim has worked in a generation company specializing in combined heat and power (CHP) schemes. In 1990 he won the National Energy Manager of the Year award for achievements in the NHS.

Richard Aylard joined Thames Water in 2002. As External Affairs and Environment Director he is a member of the board and reports to the chief executive. Richard has a particular interest in the effective communication of issues relating to sustainability, and in developing constructive dialogue and partnerships between businesses and non-governmental organizations.

Peter Bonfield is Managing Director of BRE Construction, a division of Building Research Establishment Limited, which is a wholly owned subsidiary of the BRE Trust. BRE aims to be a best-practice exemplar in its business and to become recognized worldwide as providing leadership in sustainability, innovation and safety in the built environment.

Ian Bretman is Deputy Director of the Fairtrade Foundation. The Foundation is an independent body that certifies products via the FAIRTRADE mark, a consumer label which provides an independent guarantee of a better deal for farmers and workers in the developing world.

Keith Brierley is a member of the Environment Agency's greenhouse gas emissions trading team. His responsibilities include policy matters and external communications.

The Chartered Institute of Purchasing and Supply (CIPS) is the leading international body representing purchasing and supply management professionals. It is the worldwide centre of excellence on purchasing and supply management issues. CIPS has over 400,000 members in 120 different countries, including senior business people, high-ranking civil servants and leading academics. The activities of purchasing and supply chain professionals can have a major impact on the profitability and efficiency of all types of organization.

Nick Cliffe joined the Forestry Stewardship Council (FSC) UK as Marketing Communications Manager in 2003 and became Director in mid-2005. During his time at FSC he has worked intensively on the FSC on-product labelling system, how it relates to green labelling legislation and how FSC can help the public and private sectors meet their sustainable procurement targets. Previously Nick worked in socially responsible investment and publishing.

Jon Foreman is Industry Codes and Waste Minimization Adviser to the Environment Agency. He has over 20 years' experience in waste management and regulation. Prior to the formation of the Environment Agency in 1996, Jon worked for the Hereford and Worcester Waste Regulation Authority and was responsible for the environmental management and regulation of the waste sector. He has specialized in hazardous waste management, and from the early 1990s became involved in industry waste minimization and resource efficiency programmes.

Anna Francis is a former member of the management team at Waste Watch Environmental Consultancy (WWEC, formerly Wastebusters), managed by Waste Watch Services, the trading arm of the national charity Waste Watch, which promotes waste reduction, reuse and recycling. WWEC provides expertise and practical advice to all types of organization.

Jim Gray is the Environment Agency's policy lead on modernizing regulation. Prior to joining the Environment Agency in 1999, he had 20 years' experience working in industry on regulatory policy and compliance with complex and simple regulation.

Conrad Haigh is Transport for London's Workplace Travel Planning Manager and has been working in the field of travel planning and sustainable transport promotion for eight years. In his present role he directs a team of 11 sub-regional travel plan coordinators, who are responsible for implementing travel plans in organizations across London's 33 boroughs. He is also a board member of the UK's Association for Commuter Transport.

Ruth Hounslow is Head of Marketing and Communications at Manpower UK. Established in the UK in 1956, Manpower is the UK's leading employment services company, specializing in permanent, temporary and contract recruitment, employee assessment and selection, training, outplacement, outsourcing and consulting. Manpower works with organizations in both the public and the private sector and is focused on raising productivity through improved quality, efficiency and cost reduction, enabling customers to concentrate on their core business.

Rachel Jackson is Head of Social and Environmental Issues at ACCA, the largest and fastest-growing international accountancy body, with over 320,000 students and members in 160 countries served by more than 70 staffed offices and other centres. ACCA has been actively involved with the unfolding debate on corporate social and environmental responsibility since 1990, promoting transparency and best practice. ACCA aims to help businesses and organizations realize the growing importance of sustainability to them and has launched a number of high-profile initiatives.

Graham Leigh is a former Senior Policy Officer of the Charities Aid Foundation (CAF). CAF works with companies of all sizes to help them to design and implement their corporate community investment (CCI) programmes. CAF also runs the annual Companies and Communities Awards, which are designed to recognize organizations that are shaping the future of CCI. Companies proud of their community programme are welcome to enter the CAF awards programme. Details may be found online at www.cafonline.org/cci.

Lynn Morgan is a chartered town planner with extensive experience in the development, implementation and monitoring of travel plans. She has provided travel plan advice to a range of public and private sector organizations and has also led the development of a number of travel plan Good Practice Guides on behalf of the Department for Transport and Transport for London.

Tom Morton is Managing Director of Climate Care, which raises funds by selling greenhouse gas emission reductions (referred to as CO_2 offsets). It then develops projects that reduce emissions, ensuring that the total reductions achieved match the amounts sold. Climate Care has a wide client base of over 100 ranging from large corporates to SMEs and individuals, all of whom tend to offset the emissions from their flying, driving or processes. Alternatively, they offset emissions on behalf of their customers and stakeholders for promotional reasons.

Jacqui O'Keeffe heads the Environment and Safety Group at Simmons & Simmons. Identified in Legal 500 and Chambers as a leader in her field, she has advised on a wide range of regulatory issues and projects, including Public Private Partnerships (PPP)/Private Finance Initiative (PFI), and has a particular interest in energy and climate change issues, waste and producer responsibility, contaminated land and remediation projects.

Tim Price is the Marketing Planner at Severnside Recycling. A graduate of Sheffield University, he joined the company in 2000 to work on the successful roll-out of the 'Recycling Force' – a mobile compaction fleet dedicated to the collection of recyclable packaging materials. Currently, Tim is heavily involved in the marketing of Severnside's new Facilities Management arm. Severnside Recycling is part of the DS Smith Group, the largest integrated paper and packaging group in the UK. Recyclable fibre is recovered, through its total waste facilities management services, to provide the material for the group's operations, St Regis Paper Company and DS Smith Packaging.

Greg Pritchard is the Senior Partner of CPA Audit UK, an independent consultancy based in the City of London that advises on regulatory compliance, internal audit, risk management and corporate governance issues.

Karl Russek joined ACE European Group in 2005 from his position as Vice President, ACE Environmental Risk at ACE INA in the United States. He has responsibility for launching ACE's environmental risk business across Europe, through the formation of an environmental underwriting unit that provides environmental liability products and services. Karl holds a BSc in secondary education from the University of Scranton and an MSc in environmental quality science from the University of Alaska School of Engineering.

Dan Ryan is a member of the Waste Neutral team, responsible for external communications and education. The Eden Project is an environmental education charity whose public face is the popular visitor destination situated in a former disused china clay pit in Cornwall, which has attracted over 7 million visitors since opening in 2001. The mission of the Eden Trust is to promote greater understanding of human dependence on natural resources and on the need to balance use with effective stewardship – the core message of sustainability. Dan was assisted in the compilation of his chapter by contributions from colleagues Alison Vaughan, Pat Hudson and Caron Thompson.

John Sabapathy is a researcher, writer, editor, Senior Associate of AccountAbility and Editor of its magazine *AccountAbility Forum*. He has worked for almost a decade with companies, governments and civil-society groups in the field of organizational accountability, sustainability standards and sustainable development, including five years at AccountAbility where he was Senior Research Manager until 2004, and previously at the New Economics Foundation (nef) where he was a social auditor and researcher.

James Samuel is an Associate in the Environment and Safety Group at Simmons & Simmons. He has recently spent six months on secondment at Shell International, advising Shell chemicals companies on various matters. James has assisted with a range of environmental law issues, including advising on the requirements of the Waste from Electrical and Electronic Equipment (WEEE) and Restriction of Hazardous Substances (RoHS) Directives.

Julie Smith is an Associate in the Environment and Safety Group at Simmons & Simmons. Before this she worked as an environment scientist for Southern Water. Her recent experience has covered a broad spectrum of environmental matters, including advising on the renewables obligation, the EU Emissions Trading Scheme and the Kyoto Protocol flexible mechanisms.

Errol Taylor is the Deputy Chief Executive of RoSPA, one of the world's most influential safety charities. RoSPA campaigns to prevent accidents at work, in the home, on the road, on the water and at leisure. RoSPA shares best practice through its thriving training, consultancy, audit, publications and conference businesses. Errol enjoys motoring, racquet sports, sailing and cycling.

James Taylor is a Senior Associate in the Environment and Safety Group at Simmons & Simmons. He has wide experience of environmental and health and safety matters including liability for contaminated land, waste management, waste- and defence-related PFIs, permitting and licensing, prosecutions for workplace accidents, asbestos exposure and regulatory investigations.

Unilever has a specific corporate mission to get more out of life. Unilever's environmental strategy is focused primarily on achieving its goals through eco-efficiency in its products and through three sustainability initiatives in agriculture, fish and water, areas that are directly relevant to the company.

Foreword

This book sheds light on an area which has become a critical consideration for business in the 21st century. The concepts of sustainable development and 'the sustainable enterprise' are commanding increasing public attention in the UK, and all the advanced industrialized countries. The huge impact that business can have in today's world, with the continuous growth of economic activity, the spread of globalization and the advance of technology, is increasingly being recognized. It shapes our lives and it shapes our environment. Accordingly, the issues are getting higher and higher up the boardroom agenda.

Of course, the primary goal of all businesses – to generate profit – remains unchanged. Any business that loses sight of that isn't going to be around long enough to influence the environment one way or another. But contrary to popular opinion, few boardrooms nowadays single-mindedly pursue profit to the exclusion of all other considerations. The average board has a far higher sense of social responsibility than most people realise. Directors live and raise families in the same world as everyone else.

What has also become clear is that socially responsible, environmentally friendly policies need not be in conflict with the pursuit of commercial goals. Quite the opposite. As public awareness changes, so too does the attitude of customers, shareholders and employees. This means that businesses not only have to pursue policies that command confidence and support, they also have to ensure that those policies are well communicated and fully understood. This book offers advice and guidance in preparing and implementing programmes and policies appropriate for the different contexts in which companies operate.

I believe this book will assist business people from all types of companies in understanding the business case for sustainable development. Furthermore, it will actively help them in their efforts to build and operate their own companies as sustainable enterprises. I commend this book to you.

Miles Templeman
Director General
Institute of Directors

Preface

Sustainability has become a broad church in which the congregation ranges from governments to multinational corporations, from non-governmental organizations to medium-sized and small companies and from aid charities to private individuals. On a global scale, high-profile sustainability issues include the development of food production in sub-Saharan Africa, global warming, the containment and treatment of pandemics, and toxic waste disposal. At a corporate level, even the smallest business is touched by issues such as environmental regulation, standardization and business standards, occupational health and safety, traffic congestion, land and energy use, waste management and corporate social responsibility.

In this second edition of *The Sustainable Enterprise* we focus on the corporate-level issues that are of concern to company directors in framing strategy and policy and in operating their businesses to profit from best practice. In most fields of commercial activity the attention paid to sustainability issues is no longer a matter of choice; businesses are circumscribed by a myriad of regulations, sometimes inspired at source by supranational bodies such as the G8, which are translated into EU law and EC directives that are mandatory upon the 25 member states of the European Union. Individual national governments in turn support EU regulations with their own legislation and, in many cases, add controls that increase the body of restrictions to which private industry, as well as government departments and agencies, is subject.

Mindful of the body of regulations that impact company directors and managers at all levels, we have organized this new edition into five parts, which are intended to address the key areas where sustainability and the controls that it has spawned impact business decisions most strongly. Each part includes a series of legal overviews, 14 in total, which summarize concisely the nature and scope of legislation and controls. The legal overviews are written by a team of Simmons & Simmons lawyers, whose specialist expertise covers these areas. Readers will be able to identify the issues that impact their businesses most severely and where more detailed professional advice may be required.

Part 1 covers the broader issues of sustainability where regulation and standardization have become most pervasive. The topics range from environmental regulation and emission and contamination standards to environmental and sustainability reporting. In Part 2, key aspects of business management impacted by sustainability are addressed, including risk management, supplier diversity, process efficiency and funding and investment.

Part 3 is devoted to issues in transport, health and safety and employment from a corporate viewpoint. Corporate social responsibility (CSR) today is allied strongly to sustainable issues, and Part 4 discusses specific areas in which CSR is one of the main drivers in developing better relations between business and community stakeholders.

Finally, in Part 5, our contributors write on particular environmental topics that affect all companies at a national level in the forward planning and conduct of their businesses. Part 5 concludes by addressing the practical issue of auditing in environmental management.

I take this opportunity of expressing my sincere thanks to all the authors who have contributed to the writing of this book, whose expertise and experience in their particular fields are profiled briefly in the Contributors' notes. Our thanks are also extended to the sponsors and advertisers who make the publication of this book viable.

Jonathan Reuvid

1

Regulation and standards for sustainable issues

Complying with your **environmental obligations** can **save you money** and keep your business activity **within the law...**

...It pays to know what legislation affects your business. Smaller firms can often overlook their environmental obligations and there may be a heavy price to pay if you get caught. The good news is that help is available to small businesses to ensure you do not fall foul of environmental law - and perhaps boost your credentials at the same time. The NetRegs website (www.netregs.gov.uk) was set up in response to demand from businesses for clear and consistent information.

It provides guidance in plain language on the environmental legislation that applies to small businesses and simple measures you can take to comply - many of which can lead to business efficiency savings.

It is free to use, regularly updated and with no need to register, it is completely anonymous. The website is categorised by industry sector and structured so you can easily find the information that applies to you.

Visit www.netregs.gov.uk
Guiding small businesses through environmental regulations

Sustainable value: legal overview

Julie Smith, Simmons & Simmons

There is no legal standard against which sustainable value can be measured, but as a concept it is underpinned by many issues that are subject to legislation and regulation. This can be at an international and national level, for example climate change and biodiversity. Although a consensus has been slow to emerge about the connections between corporate objectives and social and environmental objectives, recognition that businesses have responsibilities to a wide group of stakeholders is gradually gaining acceptance. It is this relationship that underpins the concept of corporate social responsibility (CSR).

CSR has developed as a way of encouraging organizations to take broader social and environmental issues into account in their day-to-day operating activities. CSR has advanced rapidly since the mid-1990s when it first began to gain widespread attention. Initially it was focused more on revenue and cost benefits, but growing awareness of the importance of reputational issues and how a poor record on environmental matters could adversely affect a company's standing and business prospects has broadened the definition.

The British Standards Institution is developing standards on CSR and sustainable development. The first of these, BS 8900 (Guidance for managing sustainable development), offers organizations clear, practical advice for making a meaningful contribution to sustainable development, and was published in May 2006.

The International Organization for Standardization is currently developing an International Standard for social responsibility, due to be published in 2008 as ISO 26000. The objective is to produce 'a guidance document, written in plain language which is understandable and usable by non-specialists' and not intended for use in certification.

In July 2002 the European Commission (EC) issued a Communication on Corporate Social Responsibility, which emphasized the voluntary nature of CSR but supported the creation of a Multi-Stakeholder Forum on CSR to discuss the issues and provide advice. The report of the Multi-Stakeholder Forum was published in June 2004 and concludes that there is no need for EC rules on CSR and that the approach to reporting on environmental and community activities should remain voluntary.

The UK's Operating and Financial Review (OFR) involves some consideration of sustainable value in that it requires a more forward-looking view of the business prospects. Climate change is specifically mentioned as an example of something that should be considered. However, the government's initial decision to abolish the OFR, followed by a reversal of its position, by announcing instead a consultation on the future of the OFR, has created some uncertainty on the exact nature and scope of current environmental reporting requirements. Companies will still need to report on environmental issues though in order to comply with the EU Accounts Modernization Directive.

Environmental regulation in the 21st century

Jim Gray, Environment Agency

New approaches to meeting this century's environmental challenges are needed in ways that make sense for the business world as well as the environment. The Environment Agency, the leading environmental regulator in England and Wales, has responded to this challenge of balancing society's demand for high environmental standards with the need to avoid putting unnecessary burdens on business. We are developing an approach to 21st-century regulation that we believe will protect the environment and human health more effectively.

Background

Traditionally, environmental regulation has been about prohibition, prescription and control. Beginning with the first Alkali Act in 1863, this approach delivered substantial benefits for people and the environment. In the last century the Clean Air Acts saved city dwellers from deadly smogs, and other pollution laws have resulted in cleaner rivers, land and air.

Direct regulation of this kind has controlled abstractions from and emissions to the environment. Such controls will continue to play an important role but will become smarter through the use of risk-based approaches, greater standardization and intelligent charging mechanisms. This will allow us to target our efforts more effectively by taking action that is more proportionate to the potential risks.

These approaches represent a new stage on the regulatory journey, moving on from a traditional command-and-control approach to a framework that provides incentives for good environmental performance and offers dialogue with business instead of instruction. *Delivering for the Environment: A 21st century approach to regulation*, published by the Environment Agency in 2005, explains in detail how we are modernizing the way we are regulating businesses.

Modernizing regulation

We are working with the Department for Environment, Food and Rural Affairs (Defra) on a joint strategy for this new approach. The priorities are:

■ reviewing existing legislation;
■ influencing the development of new EU legislation;
■ identifying inefficiencies and making changes;
■ focusing on environmental results.

There is wide acceptance that good regulation is good for business. In November 2005 the Network of Heads of European Environment Protection Agencies published a paper entitled *The Contribution of Good Environmental Regulation to Competitiveness*, referred to as 'the Prague Statement', which reviews the evidence on the links between environmental regulation and competitiveness. The paper provides many examples of how environmental regulation benefits business as well as the environment. It finds that effective environmental regulation drives innovation, fosters new markets and reduces business risks. It also encourages competitiveness and sustainable economic development.

Recently there has been increasing emphasis on the need to reduce administrative burdens on business, and we are working with Defra on their plan to slash unnecessary red tape by simplifying regulation. Work has already started to better understand, manage and reduce the administrative burden we place on industry. The aim of modernizing regulation is to provide more effective ways of achieving a sustainable and improving environment – benefiting us and the businesses we regulate. We will encourage businesses to improve, rewarding good performers while remaining tough on those that do not meet acceptable standards. We will use dialogue to solve problems jointly with industry, and will focus on the desired environmental improvement rather than the regulatory process.

Modernizing regulation focuses on the potential environmental risk of an activity. We have to be thorough in assessing environmental risks and then regulate in a proportionate way. We have, for example, worked with government in England and Wales to allow an estimated 500,000 low-risk hazardous waste producers not to register with us, saving them at least £9 million a year. From May 2005 we made electronic registration available for those that do need to register. To date, 80 per cent of the 220,000 registrations have been in electronic form. From 1 April 2005 we have taken holders of 23,000 low-risk abstraction licences out of the licensing regime, saving them approximately £1 million per year.

Business benefits

By focusing our inspection and enforcement activities on the biggest risks, without neglecting less significant risks, we will maximize the impact of our effort to achieve a better environment. Focusing on the biggest risks also makes sense for businesses that manage their risks well, because they will be subject to less intrusive regulation. On the other hand, those that do not take their environmental responsibilities seriously will see more of our inspectors until they improve their environmental performance.

Business needs to be more aware of how its actions impact on the environment and human health. Education and advice raise awareness and offer solutions. We have recently received funding to develop further our NetRegs website, which provides simple, tailored guidance for 105 business sectors and attracts over 2 million 'hits' each year.

Importantly for businesses, our charges will reflect environmental risk, including the operator's performance in managing the site. Risk is determined by several factors, not just the intrinsic hazard of an activity or plant. This is where environmental management systems and procedures can reduce the risk of environmental accidents.

We believe that a well-planned and well-implemented environmental management system will help to improve the management of environmental risks from a site or activity and therefore the risk will be reduced. The effectiveness of companies' environmental management systems or procedures will be part of our assessment for judging what does and does not constitute 'real' risk. By identifying, managing and reducing key risk areas, businesses can reduce their risk profile, which will then be reflected in lower charges and reduced compliance assessment.

That good environmental performance goes hand in hand with good business performance has been well documented. Going green can actually enhance a company's commercial standing. In today's world, business, industries and individuals are expected to take responsibility for environmental performance and regulatory compliance. Businesses and industries with environmentally aware practices are prospering and making savings. In addition, businesses can usually benefit from savings in raw materials and waste disposal costs. For example, being energy efficient and reducing waste could save business and industry £5.8 billion annually.

Modernizing regulation in practice

Direct regulation through permits, consents and licences will remain a fundamental part of our work but will be streamlined wherever possible. Direct regulation may also be used to underpin trading and voluntary agreements to make sure that participants meet a minimum level of performance. Voluntary or negotiated agreements work best in mature, well-managed sectors with a history of regulatory compliance or a 'good reputation' to uphold. They can be useful where a large number of very similar activities or sites need to be controlled. Trading schemes such as the Emissions Trading Scheme, and economic instruments such as environmental taxes, for example the Climate Change Levy and landfill tax, are also part of the modernizing approach and have an important part to play in protecting our environment.

Modernizing regulation means using the best tools for the job rather than a blanket approach regardless of the nature and scale of the environmental risk.

We have developed a wider and smarter range of tools for assessing regulatory compliance, including operator and pollution risk appraisal (OPRA) schemes, compliance assessment schemes and a sector planning approach.

A better toolbox

When we regulate we are focused on the environmental results we want to achieve. Sector plans were developed for the key industrial sectors detailing what we want to achieve. We published sector plans for the cement, nuclear and chemical sectors in November 2005. We are now developing plans for the waste, water, power generation, dairy and food and drink sectors.

Our approach to permitting is also being modernized by moving towards a common model for permits, using standard templates and rules where appropriate rather than having a bespoke permit at each site. We adapt the standard approach with site-specific conditions where necessary, but greater standardization means we can ensure a consistent approach to regulatory requirements throughout England and Wales, while saving our own resources and those of the businesses seeking permits.

There is only so far we can go with this approach under current legislation. We are working with government in England and Wales on the Environmental Permitting Programme, which aims to streamline, modernize and simplify existing legislation to provide a framework approach that will enable us to use a standard permitting approach more extensively. Stakeholders are fully involved in this programme of work, and new legislation will be widely consulted on before being laid before Parliament.

The OPRA schemes are a good example of modern regulation in practice. This risk assessment tool helps us to formalize judgements about environmental risks, using a standardized scoring system that takes into account the key elements of risk: operator performance and environmental hazard. It allows us to allocate resources and set charges based on the risk involved. Originally developed for large industrial sites, OPRA has been adapted for waste management sites, and now environmental protection OPRA applies to sites under the Integrated Pollution Prevention and Control regime. Our compliance assessment efforts are directed to activities that have a high OPRA score.

We have also developed a compliance classification tool, which allows us to classify permit breaches more consistently. We are working with government in England and Wales on the review of penalty regimes to make sure that our enforcement action can be sufficient to deter persistent offenders.

These examples illustrate our proportionate, risk-based approach. We do not want to stifle business innovation and growth, but 21st-century citizens expect products and services to be delivered responsibly and safely. Modernizing regulation aims to find the right balance between these two objectives. It will encourage environmental improvements and reward good performance, but still provide the ultimate reassurance that tough action will be taken on those that fail to meet acceptable standards.

Delivering for the Environment: A 21st century approach to regulation can be found on the Environment Agency website at www.environment-agency.gov.uk/business.

Standards and sustainability

Errol Taylor, The Royal Society for the Prevention of Accidents (RoSPA)

The business case

'New standards can be the source of enormous wealth, or the death of corporate empires' – a perspective that is often overlooked by many executives, who see standards and standardization as being synonymous with bureaucracy and red tape. In the fight for commercial survival, where sustainability is about hitting profit and turnover targets, wider issues such as the enhancement of social, human, manufactured and natural capital are often left as a secondary priority.

This is probably a reflection of the origins of the most widely adopted standard, ISO 9001. At the height of the United Kingdom's Thatcher revolution, when Japanese manufacturers were leading the way with consistently cheaper and better products, the UK Ministry of Defence and many government departments started to ask suppliers to be certified to BS 5750, the forerunner of ISO 9001. The quality industry was born, with a new breed of consultants and auditors. They gave organizations clear methodologies for documenting activities, and the result was a step-change improvement in quality control.

Most executives embark on the journey towards compliance with and certification to standards as a leap of faith, since it is very difficult to demonstrate any direct linkage between financial performance and the use of standards. However, Corbett *et al* reviewed the performance of over 300 US companies in three industrial sectors (electronics, chemicals and industrial machinery) and demonstrated that certified organizations improved their return on assets at a higher rate than those that were not certified (see Figure 1.3.1).

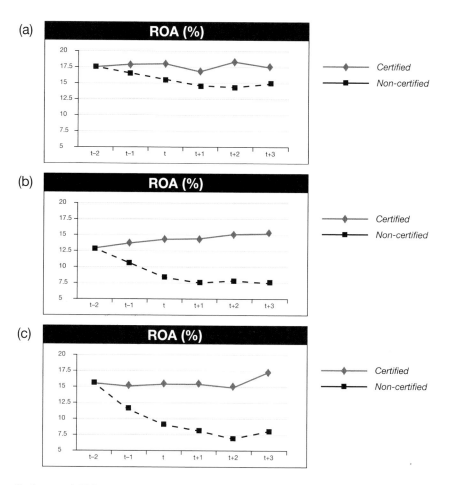

Source: Corbett *et al*, *ISO Management Systems*, July–August 2002

Figure 1.3.1 Does ISO 9000 certification pay? ISO 9000 certification in (a) the chemical industry (SIC 28); (b) the industrial machinery and computer industry (SIC 35); (c) the electronic equipment and components industry (SIC 36)

Maybe surprisingly, the positive business case also applies to small to medium-sized enterprises (see Figure 1.3.2). Traditionally, entrepreneurs see compliance with regulations as a necessary evil. However, a common pattern for two- to four-year-old businesses is to adopt certification as part of their growth strategy.

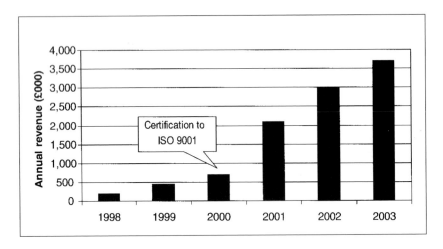

Figure 1.3.2   Growth of a successful small or medium-sized enterprise (SME)

By this stage, they will have saturated their local, start-up market and need to grow either geographically or by appealing to large national and multinational potential clients. For these organizations, certification is useful shorthand proving that the business can manage its fundamental processes effectively and is likely to be a reliable supplier.

Other organizations recognize that the process of standardization can be used to create new markets and exclude some (or all) of their competitors. In fiercely competitive industries such as consumer electronics, manufacturers are constantly fighting to dominate the market with their patented products and services. An industry standard can give significant competitive advantage to certain participants, thereby creating the need for organizations such as the British Standards Institution (BSI) to consult widely in the development of standards that are in the public good as well as being beneficial to individual companies.

A strong philosophical argument is that standardization should help build sustainable futures for communities and organizations by finding common ground among interested parties. The quarry or waste treatment plant that ignores the needs of the local villagers is unlikely to remain in business for long: unacceptable levels of noise, dirt, smell and toxic effluent are likely to cause a storm of protest, leading at best to increased security costs and at worst to closure of the operation and redundancies for the workforce.

The roles of standards and standardization

Today's executives face a bewildering array of standards and codes of practice. Their origins can be instructive: ISO 9001 and ISO 14001 were developed as genuine attempts to help organizations improve the quality of their products and reduce their impact on the environment, respectively. In contrast, financial scandals affecting pensions and shareholder value have led to a series of corporate governance reviews, starting with the Cadbury Report and culminating in the inclusion of Higgs's recommendations in the London Stock Exchange's Combined Code.

The UK has pioneered standardization as a means of providing a level playing field for organizations to compete freely in national and international markets while generally improving quality of life for all concerned. Although there is plenty of room for further improvement, the UK is a world leader in the field of risk management and has an enviable safety record in the home, on the road and in the workplace.

Compliance with publicly available specifications (such as Kitemark schemes) provides reassurance to specifiers, buyers and users that the product is safe and its performance will exceed the minimum specified. As a result, injuries due to faulty building materials, toys and electrical goods are now the exception rather than the rule.

RoSPA's active campaigning for the adoption of compulsory seatbelts, banning the use of hand-held mobile phones and widespread use of unpopular speed cameras at accident blackspots has helped to cut the number of fatalities of motorists and pedestrians despite ever-increasing levels of vehicle usage, as Figure 1.3.3 demonstrates.

Despite this, it is sobering to think that a motorist driving more than 25,000 miles per year has the same risk profile as a deep-sea diver. Employees are five times more likely to die on the road, while driving as part of their job, than they are of suffering a fatal accident in the workplace. Guidance such as RoSPA's 'Managing occupational road risk' (MORR™) encourages managers to review a wide range of factors, including

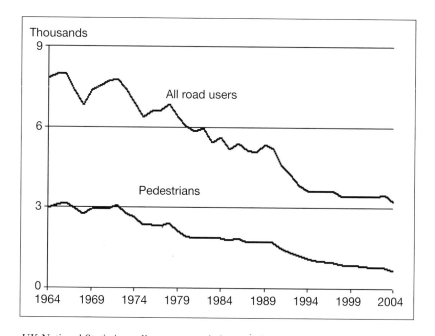

Source: UK National Statistics online, www.statistics.gov.uk

Figure 1.3.3   Decline in deaths of road users

corporate culture, management attitude and targets, and accident history, as well as the risk profile of individual drivers, to minimize occupational road risk.

The Health and Safety Executive's (HSE) guidance, HSG65, together with BS 8800, provides managers with a clear framework for managing the health and safety of employees in the workplace. Tools such as the audit specification, OHSAS 18001 (based on BS 8800), and RoSPA's QSA (which embodies OHSAS 18001 and HSG65) can be used to measure compliance. QSA has the added benefit of allowing benchmarking of numerical results to drive continuous improvement. The Health and Safety at Work Act 1974 (HSWA74) provides the legislative backbone that encourages directors and senior managers to take their responsibilities seriously. Taken together with robust enforcement by HSE inspectors, the trend in workplace fatalities speaks for itself. Organizations now focus on differentiating their particular combination of products and services to gain market advantage rather than cutting dangerous corners.

Whilst directors of small organizations have been successfully prosecuted using the HSWA74, various high-profile actions against large organizations have failed (such as P&O, in relation to the capsize of the *Herald of Free Enterprise*) because of the need to demonstrate that a 'controlling mind' was responsible. This is hard to prove where there are multiple layers of management and shared responsibility. The Corporate Manslaughter Bill should make it easier to prosecute organizations where 'there is evidence of serious management failure involving behaviour falling far below what might reasonably be expected'. Well-managed organizations should have nothing to fear: the bill is aimed at the minority of criminally negligent management teams. The bill therefore protects the majority of organizations by dealing with the minority of unscrupulous and dangerous operators.

In the hi-tech industries such as telecoms and software engineering, the protection of intellectual property has become absolutely paramount: Microsoft's Windows source code can be copied on to a standard CD ROM and would be of immense value to criminals throughout the world trying to gain access to banking details on personal computers. The reputation and ongoing sustainability of all service businesses depends on their clients having total faith in the businesses' ability to manage confidential information and keep it secret. At a more fundamental level, market research findings are often controversial, and marketers have to be creative in selectively using the data. Any leaking of the full facts could have a devastating effect on the organization, as can be testified by unfortunate business leaders like Gerald Ratner (who unfavourably compared his best-selling carriage clock with a prawn sandwich).

The SIGMA Project 3 – Sustainability: Integrated Guidelines for Management – was launched in 1999 by BSI, Forum for the Future (a leading sustainability charity and think tank) and AccountAbility (an international professional body for account-ability), with the support of the UK Department of Trade and Industry (DTI). The SIGMA project developed the SIGMA Management Framework to provide clear, practical advice to organizations to enable them to make a meaningful contribution to sustainable development. Underpinning the SIGMA Management Framework are the Guiding Principles, which consist of the two core elements of holistic management and accountability.

Holistic management of five different types of capital reflects an organization's overall impact and wealth. The five capitals are as follows:

■ *Natural capital* is the natural resources (energy and matter) and processes needed by organizations to produce their products and deliver their services. These include sinks that absorb, neutralize or recycle wastes; resources, some of which are renewable, while others are not; and processes, such as climate regulation and the carbon cycle, that enable life to continue in a balanced and healthy way.

■ *Social capital* is any value added to the activities and economic outputs of an organization by human relationships, partnerships and cooperation. Social capital includes, for example, networks, communication channels, families, communities, businesses, trade unions, schools and voluntary organizations, as well as cultural and social norms, values and trust.

■ *Human capital* incorporates the health, knowledge, skills, intellectual outputs, motivation and capacity for relationships of the individual. In an organizational context it includes the elements needed for human beings to engage in productive work and the creation of wealth, thereby achieving a better quality of life.

■ *Manufactured capital* is material goods and infrastructure owned, leased or controlled by an organization that contribute to production or service provision, but do not become embodied in its output.

■ *Financial capital* reflects the productive power and value of the other four types of capital and covers those assets of an organization that exist in a form of currency that can be owned or traded, including (but not limited to) shares, bonds and banknotes.

All the capitals are heavily interlinked, and there is some overlap between them. This whole system is then encircled by the principle of accountability, representing the relationship that an organization has with the outside world – with its stakeholders and for its stewardship of the five capitals.

The SIGMA Management Framework describes a four-phase cycle to manage and embed sustainability issues within core organizational processes (see Figure 1.3.4). Organizations may enter the cycle at different points and work through the phases at different speeds according to their particular circumstances and existing systems.

Selecting the best fit for your organization

'Triple bottom line' reporting, covering social, environmental and economic issues, is becoming the norm for many organizations. Listed in Table 1.3.1 are some of today's main management standards, with an indication of their relevance to elements of the 'triple bottom line'. Generally, these standards are common-sense lists of best current management practice. In some cases they are aspirations, outlining 'next' management practice and therefore giving organizations a clear sense of direction.

By their nature, standards have little to offer that is unusual, unexpected or in-appropriate. The challenge for most organizations is how to prioritize their adoption, given the plethora of conflicting pressures they face from stakeholders.

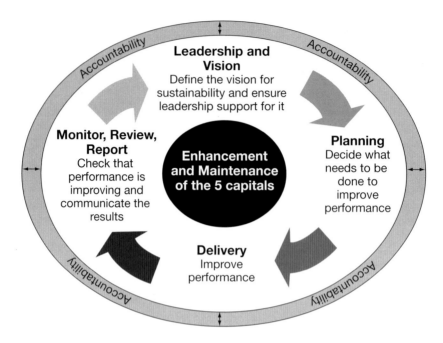

Figure 1.3.4   Embedding sustainability issues within core organizational processes

The Systems Prioritization Matrix (SPM) (Figure 1.3.5, page 20) was developed to help managers and directors decide whether a management system would add value to their organization by using a simple, four-stage process:

- *Stage 1:* List all the systems that you are aware of. The list given in Figure 1.3.5 is for illustrative purposes and is not intended to be exhaustive.
- *Stage 2:* Consider all the external drivers requiring compliance or certification to the system. If the organization is an engineering company supplying the automotive supply chain, it will probably be required to have certified quality and environmental systems. To capture this information, a score of between 1 and 5 has to be allocated. The top score of 5 applies where there are very strong external drivers, such as a customer mandate. The bottom score of 1 is where external drivers are weak or non-existent.
- *Stage 3:* Repeat stage 2, but this time consider each system from an internal perspective. How valuable is certification to ISO 14001 in helping the organization position itself and generate additional revenues by claiming to be particularly environmentally friendly in an industry that is seen as having a poor pollution record? How could demonstration of excellent procedures for business continuity and protection of intellectual property help a software developer win new contracts from blue-chip clients? Would compliance to HSG65 or OHSAS 18001 help demonstrate high levels of health and safety to sceptical stakeholders, such as the

Table 1.3.1 Some of today's main management standards

Title of Management System or Framework	Description	Name or Number	Linkage to the Triple Bottom Line				Strategic Context on the Route to Sustainability
			Social	Environ-mental	Eco-nomic		
Sustainability: Integrated Guidelines for Management	Integration of social, environmental and business issues	SIGMA	✓	✓	✓		Management consolidation. Basic needs met
Corporate Governance	Compliance by executives and non-executives with the Combined Code	UK Combined Code (Higgs, Cadbury et al)	✓	✓	✓		Governance and strategy
Managing Risk through Corporate Governance	Guide to help identify business risks and their likelihood together with controls as part of corporate governance requirements	PD 6668	✓	✓	✓		Governance & strategy
EU Eco-Management and Audit Scheme (EMAS)	Allows companies to evaluate, report and improve their environmental performance	EMAS		✓	✓		Stakeholder engagement and reporting
Environmental Management	Environmental performance evaluation – guidelines	ISO 14031		✓	✓		Stakeholder engagement and reporting

Table 1.3.1 Some of today's main management standards (*continued*)

Title of Management System or Framework	Description	Name or Number	Linkage to the Triple Bottom Line			Strategic Context on the Route to Sustainability
			Social	Environ-mental	Eco-nomic	
Accountability	A framework to improve accountability and performance by learning through stakeholder engagement	AA 1000	✓			Stakeholder engagment
BPIR	Business Performance Improvement Review – stakeholder review and prioritization using the principles of ISO 9004	BPIR	✓		✓	Stakeholder engagment
Business continuity	Review the way your organization provides its products and services and increase its resilience to disruption, interruption or loss	PAS 56	✓		✓	Corporate responsibility and licence to operate
Social Accountability	A tool for retailers, brand companies, suppliers and other organizations to ensure just and decent working conditions in the supply chain	SA 8000	✓			Corporate responsibility and licence to operate

Name	Description	Code				
European Quality Award	The EFQM Excellence Model was introduced at the beginning of 1992 as the framework for assessing applications for the European Quality Award	EFQM	✓	✓	✓	Growth stage
Quality Management System	The international certifiable standard for quality management systems: the fundamental process-based approach on which other systems can be built	2000	✓		✓	Formalization of management systems leading to growth stage
Information Security	Ensures that your organization effectively manages the risks attached to your information data systems	BS 7799			✓	Legal compliance
Occupational Health & Safety	Occupational Health and Safety Management System (OHSMS) helps risk management strategy to assess changing legislation and to protect the workforce	OHSAS 18001	✓			Legal compliance
Environmental Management System	The international certifiable standard for environmental management systems: a risk-based approach	ISO 14001		✓		Legal compliance
Investors in People	Sets a level of good practice for improving an organization's performance through its people	IIP	✓			Formalization of management systems
Acorn	A five- to six-phase approach to help SMEs implement an EMS in line with ISO 14001 or EMAS	BS 8555		✓		Formalization of management systems

Systems Prioritization Matrix				
Management System	A External priority	B Internal priority	A × B	Rank
Quality				
Environmental				
Occupational health and safety				
Information security				
Business continuity				
Staff motivation				
Social/ethical				
Corporate governance				

Figure 1.3.5   The Systems Prioritization Matrix (SPM)

UK public vis-à-vis the nuclear power industry? Again, the same rationale applies, with a score of 5 where compliance or certification would be highly beneficial to the organization.

■ *Stage 4:* Multiply column A by column B, noting the scores and ranking the systems in order: systems with the highest scores clearly should be receiving higher priority and more resources.

The three worked examples in Figure 1.3.6, based on the broad primary sectors of the economy (manufacturing, process and services), show how priorities can be very different. The same applies within an organization, where the focus for one plant may be completely different from that of a call centre or the corporate headquarters. Rankings can be checked against intuitive reasoning, as follows:

■ *Manufacturers* are tightly controlled by their clients' specifications. Everything has to be geared around consistently delivering product at the right time, place and cost without causing harm or injury to anyone during the production process or during the product's useful life.

■ For *process* industries (ranging from petrochemicals to electricity generators), relatively long and stable production runs mean that quality is well controlled. Risks associated with damaging people or the environment through spillages and/ or explosions must be uppermost in the minds of senior managers.

■ Within the *services* sector, the ephemeral nature of the product means that the quality and motivation of staff at the point of delivery to the clients are absolutely critical. Clients' needs and well-being have to be top priority.

Manufacturing organizations

Management System	A External priority	B Internal priority	A × B	Rank
Quality	5	3	15	3
Environmental	4	3	12	2
Occupational health and safety	4	4	16	1
Information security	2	3	6	
Business continuity	2	2	4	
Staff motivation	1	3	3	
Social/ethical	3	2	6	
Corporate governance	3	3	9	

Process industries

Management System	A External priority	B Internal priority	A × B	Rank
Quality	2	4	8	
Environmental	5	4	20	1=
Occupational health and safety	5	4	20	1=
Information security	2	3	6	
Business continuity	3	4	12	3=
Staff motivation	1	3	3	
Social/ethical	1	2	2	
Corporate governance	4	3	12	3=

Services organizations

Management System	A External priority	B Internal priority	A × B	Rank
Quality	2	3	6	
Environmental	2	2	4	
Occupational health and safety	3	5	15	2=
Information security	4	3	12	
Business continuity	4	5	20	1
Staff motivation	3	5	15	2=
Social/ethical	2	2	4	
Corporate governance	3	4	12	

Figure 1.3.6 The Systems Prioritization Matrix (SPM): three worked examples

Conclusion

Standardization can be highly beneficial for whole economic sectors and individual organizations, creating new markets for certified organizations while excluding others. Well-written standards embody best current management practice, and in many cases they show the way forward by describing 'next' practice. Well-managed organizations tend naturally to adopt many of the requirements listed within standards. The perennial challenge for executives and their senior managers is to focus on their strategic priorities and channel finite resources to achieve sustainability.

Trading greenhouse gases

Keith Brierley, Environment Agency

The European Union's Emission Trading Scheme (EU ETS) is a key tool to achieve the reductions in greenhouse gas emissions that are essential to combat global warming. It will help the United Kingdom achieve its legal obligations under the Kyoto Protocol.

Under the EU's burden-sharing agreement, the UK's Kyoto target is a 12.5 per cent reduction on 1990 levels by the first Kyoto Protocol commitment period (2008–12).

The EU ETS will also contribute to delivering the UK's domestic goal of a 20 per cent reduction in carbon dioxide emissions below 1990 levels by 2010. The aim of emissions trading is to allow the reduction targets to be met in the most cost-effective manner.

The Environment Agency permitted a total of 822 installations under the scheme in early 2005. Of these, around 316 are opted-out installations with 23 direct participants in the UK Emissions Trading Scheme and 293 operators with climate change agreements.

How trading will work

The scheme operates by the allocation and trading of greenhouse gas emissions allowances throughout the EU. One allowance represents 1 tonne of carbon dioxide equivalent. An overall limit, or 'cap', is set by member states' governments on the total amount of emissions allowed from all the installations covered by the scheme. At the end of each year, operators are required to ensure they have enough allowances to account for their installation's emissions. They have the flexibility to buy additional allowances (on top of their free allocation) or to sell any surplus allowances generated from reducing their emissions. These options create a flexible compliance regime for operators and also ensure emissions are effectively capped across the EU.

The scheme currently has two operating phases: Phase 1 from 1 January 2005 to 31 December 2007; and Phase 2 from 1 January 2008 to 31 December 2012. Carbon dioxide emissions are the only greenhouse gas covered by the EU ETS in Phase 1.

The sectors covered by the scheme are:

■ combustion processes (with a rated thermal input exceeding 20 megawatts);
■ activities of mineral oil refineries;
■ activities of coke ovens;
■ production and processing of ferrous metals;
■ production of cement clinker or lime;
■ manufacture of glass and glass fibre;
■ manufacture of ceramic bricks;
■ production of pulp from timber or other fibrous materials;
■ manufacture of paper and board.

For more detail on installations covered by the scheme, see Table 1.4.1 (page 27).

Businesses within the scope of the EU ETS must have a greenhouse gas emissions permit – in effect, a licence to operate and emit carbon dioxide.

The following regulators issue permits:

■ Environment Agency – England and Wales;
■ Scottish Environment Protection Agency (SEPA) – Scotland;
■ Department of Environment – Northern Ireland;
■ Department of Trade and Industry (DTI) – UK offshore installations.

EU ETS permits require operators to monitor and report emissions in accordance with the Commission's guidelines for monitoring and reporting. Each year, emissions data must be verified and the equivalent number of allowances surrendered. In the UK, all transactions and surrendering of allowances take place on a national registry administered by the Environment Agency.

The approved UK National Allocation Plan (NAP) for Phase 1 was published on 24 May 2005. This set out how allowances were to be issued to UK installations covered by the scheme. The total quantity of allowances issued to UK installations for Phase 1 was 736 million, subject to the Commission's consideration of the UK's proposal to increase the total quantity of allowances in the UK NAP to 756 million.

In accordance with the requirements of the UK's NAP, allowances are issued to permit holders in February of each year in Phase 1.

For new entrants – that is, new installations and extensions to existing installations – the UK NAP includes a quantity of allowances, the New Entrant Reserve (NER), to be distributed free to qualifying installations. Applications are determined on a strict queue system administered by the Environment Agency.

From the start of 2005, businesses in the scheme have been able to buy or sell emission allowances, which provides an opportunity to make profits from trading.

At the end of each period (the first deadline having been 30 April 2006), participants in the trading scheme must hold allowances equal to all of their emissions during the period. Those allowances are then surrendered. This is how the scheme delivers the most cost-effective emission reductions. Firms will choose to buy allowances from other participants if doing so costs less than other means of staying within their allocation. On the other hand, firms that can reduce emissions relatively cheaply will do so, putting them in a position to sell surplus allowances. The desired environmental result will be achieved because the overall allocation of carbon dioxide allowances is fixed, but trading will make possible the most cost-effective route to the required reductions.

Example

A company that currently emits 100,000 tonnes equivalent receives allowances of only 90,000. If allowances were trading at 20 euros, it would cost 200,000 euros to bridge the gap (10,000 tonnes equivalent at 20 euros per tonne equivalent). If it would cost more than 200,000 euros to bring emissions within the ceiling, then it would be worth buying the extra allowances. But if emissions could be cut for less than 200,000 euros, that would be the best option.

Monitoring and verification

From 2006, operators must submit a verified report of their annual emissions to the regulator (in England and Wales, the Environment Agency) for the preceding calendar year by 31 March.

The EU has adopted monitoring and reporting guidelines that offer a choice between direct measurement and calculation of emissions. They present a range of 'tiered' methodologies, based on the level of accuracy, for each industry sector. Operators will be expected to use the highest (most accurate) tier unless that is not technically feasible or will lead to unreasonably high costs. There is limited provision within the guidelines to apply less stringent standards to minor sources within sites, namely sources that contribute less than 5 per cent of total emissions from that site.

Biomass fuels, although included in the scheme, will be zero-rated, and the following fuels are carbon neutral for the purposes of the scheme:

■ wood wastes;
■ sewage sludge;
■ biofuels;
■ landfill gas;
■ biomass fractions of paper, cardboard, municipal waste and cardboard waste.

Penalties

Penalties will apply for failing to hold a valid permit, failing to comply with monitoring and reporting conditions, or failing to have surrendered sufficient allowances (which is equivalent to producing excessive emissions).

During the first phase of the scheme, failure to have surrendered enough allowances will incur a fine of 40 euros for each excess tonne. Our example company with annual carbon dioxide emissions of 100,000 tonnes equivalent but with allowances of only 90,000 tonnes equivalent could be liable to a fine of 400,000 euros if it did not balance the books either by reducing emissions or by purchasing more allowances.

The second phase (2008–12)

The Commission's guidance on Phase 2 NAPs (published 22 January 2005) confirms that the scheme will remain focused on carbon dioxide emissions. It also seeks to harmonize the scope of the scheme across all member states by specifying the inclusion of combustion processes involving crackers, carbon black, flaring, furnaces and integrated steelworks, typically carried out in larger installations causing considerable emissions.

During this phase the fine for failing to retire sufficient allowances will rise from 40 euros to 100 euros for each excess tonne.

Further information

For further information and guidance on policy issues, visit the Defra website at http://www.defra.gov.uk/environment/climatechange/trading/eu/index.htm.

For further information and guidance on the EU ETS, including applying for an EU ETS permit in England and Wales, visit the Environment Agency website at http://environment-agency.gov.uk/emissionstrading.

Schedule 1: Installations covered by the EU Emissions Trading Scheme

The first phase covers installations that carry out any of the activities in Annex I of the EU Emissions Trading Directive.

Table 1.4.1 Summary of EU ETS Schedule 1 activities

1. Energy activities
1.1 Activities of combustion installations with a rated thermal input exceeding 20 megawatts (excluding hazardous or municipal waste installations).
1.2 Activities of mineral oil refineries.
1.3 Activities of coke ovens.
2. Production and processing of ferrous metals
2.1 Activities of metal ore (including sulphide ore) roasting and sintering installations.
2.2 Activities of installations for the production of pig iron or steel (primary or secondary fusion), including continuous casting, with a capacity of more than 2.5 tonnes per hour.
3. Mineral industries
3.1 Activities of installations for the production of cement clinker in rotary kilns with a production capacity of more than 500 tonnes per day.
3.2 Activities of installations for the production of lime in rotary kilns or other furnaces with a production capacity of more than 50 tonnes per day.
3.3 Activities of installations for the manufacture of glass, including glass fibre, where the melting capacity of the plant is more than 20 tonnes per day.
3.4 Activities of installations for the manufacture of ceramic products (including roofing tiles, bricks, refractory bricks, tiles, stoneware or porcelain) by firing in kilns where:
(i) the kiln production capacity is more than 75 tonnes per day; or
(ii) the kiln capacity is more than 4 m^3 and the setting density is more than 300 kg/m^3.
4. Other activities
4.1 Activities of industrial plants for the production of pulp from timber or other fibrous materials.
4.2 Activities of industrial plants for the production of paper and board with a production capacity of more than 20 tonnes per day.

Note: The threshold values given above generally refer to production capacities or outputs. Where one operator carries out several activities falling under the same subheading in the same installation or on the same site, the capacities of such activities are added together.

Business standards: legal overview

Jacqui O'Keeffe, Simmons & Simmons

There are many different voluntary initiatives in the corporate governance and corporate social responsibility area that an organization can adopt. These include the Equator Principles (guidelines for financial institutions funding development projects), the CERES Principles (10 principles relating specifically to environmental awareness and accountability), the Global Reporting Initiative (GRI) Sustainability Reporting Guidelines, and the Association of British Insurers (ABI) Disclosure Guidelines on Socially Responsible Investment. In March 2006, Defra published 'Environmental Key Performance Indicators – Reporting Guidelines for UK Businesses'. A draft ISO on corporate social responsibility (due to be published in 2008 as ISO 26000) is being developed, which is being designed to be consistent with ISO 9000 or ISO 14001.

Regulations came into force across the UK in April 2005 to make it mandatory for directors of a listed company to prepare an annual Operating and Financial Review (OFR). The regulations require companies to report on their environmental and social impact. The review objective is a balanced and comprehensive analysis of the development and performance of the business during the financial year, the position of the company at the end of the year, the main trends and factors underlying that development, performance and position, and the main trends and factors that are likely to affect future development, performance and position. The OFR is not intended to replace free-standing environment or sustainability reports, which it is expected will contain more detail than the OFR. However, the future of the OFR is uncertain, as the Chancellor of the Exchequer announced in November 2005 that the OFR would be abolished. Following the commencement of judicial review proceedings into this decision, the Chancellor has reversed his position and announced a consultation on the future of the OFR. In any event, the vast majority of the reporting requirements in the OFR are already included in the context of the Business Review which is part of a company's usual reporting requirements.

Environmental and sustainability reporting

Rachel Jackson, ACCA

Organizations are increasingly coming to realize that, in order to meet the growing demands made on them by their competitors, external stakeholders and the government, they need to change the way they 'do business'. This change includes becoming more open and accountable for the economic, environmental and social consequences of their activities. This new (and often underestimated) dimension of corporate governance includes taking responsibility for the full range of positive and negative consequences arising from corporate decisions and actions, and disclosing these impacts in an appropriate environmental, social and sustainability report.

Over the past decade, companies worldwide have come under increasing pressure to conduct their business in a more open and responsible manner. The following developments have been identified as the key drivers that have encouraged businesses to become more responsible:

- the increasing size and influence of companies;
- the growth of civil society activism, increasing the influence of non-governmental organizations (NGOs);
- the increased importance a company places on intangibles;
- advances in communications technology.

These developments are encouraging more businesses to question what they do and how they do it. In the early 1990s only a handful of companies were sufficiently far-thinking to publish voluntary data on their non-financial impacts. Over a decade on, the situation looks very different, with a growing number of companies reporting each year from an increasing number of countries.

These reports have become highly effective tools for communicating to stake-holders the environmental, social and wider economic performance of an organiza-tion. Estimates put the total number of environmental reports produced worldwide at around 4,000. Although environmental and sustainability reporting has yet to reach a generally accepted standard of financial reporting, there has nevertheless been a rapid evolutionary process that has contributed to the high standard of environmental and sustainability reports seen today. Mandatory environmental reporting regimes have been introduced in various parts of the world, including the Netherlands, Denmark, Australia, the United States and, most recently, France.

What is environmental reporting?

'Environmental reporting' is the term commonly used to describe the disclosure by an entity of environmentally related data, verified (audited) or not, regarding environmental risks, environmental impacts, policies, strategies, targets, costs, liabilities or environmental performance to those who have an interest in such in-formation, as an aid to enabling or enriching their relationship with the reporting entity. Disclosure can take place via:

■ the annual report;
■ a stand-alone corporate environmental performance report;
■ a site-centred environmental statement;
■ some other medium (eg staff newsletter, video, CD ROM or website).

The Sustainability Working Party of the European Federation of Accountants (FEE) defines the objective of external environmental reporting as being 'the provision of information about the environmental impact and operational performance of an entity that is useful to relevant stakeholders in assessing their relationship with the reporting entity'.

An excellent environmental report clearly acknowledges and explains the en-vironmental impacts of an organization's operations and products, and publicly demonstrates the organization's commitment to reduce them accordingly.

What is sustainability reporting?

As sustainability reporting is an emerging and rapidly developing practice, there have been several attempts to define what a sustainability report is or should be. In general, however, sustainability reporting involves reporting on the economic, environmental and social impact of organizational performance. A sustainability report should be a high-level strategic document that addresses the issues, challenges and opportunities sustainable development brings to the core business and its industry sector. All material and relevant elements of sustainability – economic, environmental and social – should be addressed, on both a separate and an integrated basis.

As a sustainability report is a strategic report, key business issues such as public policy positions, risk management procedures and governance commitment should also be disclosed. Economic indicators can include cost of all goods, materials and services purchased; total payroll and benefits expense; total sum of taxes of all types paid; and donations to community, civil-society or other groups. Social issues can include labour practices, human rights, and societal and product responsibility issues.

Reporting by small and medium-sized enterprises

It is well known that fewer small and medium-sized organizations (SMEs) disclose social, economic and environmental information than do their larger counterparts: even on a global scale, the total number of reporting organizations remains small. SMEs have fewer resources – finance, time, knowledge – available to them, which restricts the number of SMEs that report on sustainability issues.

ACCA believes in principle, however, that all businesses, in all areas of industry and of whatever size, need to address the issue of sustainable development and integrate it into their business strategies. The level of effort and expense that SMEs can devote to this will vary, however, and the special circumstances of SMEs need to be respected.

Benefits of environmental and sustainability reporting

Since environmental and sustainability reporting in most countries is a purely voluntary activity, it is necessary for companies to perceive some tangible benefits when establishing the business case to report. The following are some of the benefits most commonly cited by reporting organizations:

- Reporting demonstrates the coherence of overall management strategies to important external stakeholders.
- By disclosing management strategies, systems and policies relating to the environment and society, an organization can demonstrate to its stakeholders its holistic approach to environmental responsibility.
- Reporting assists in the aligning of corporate vision and principles with internal business practices and activities.

Strengthened stakeholder relations

One of the benefits of increasing corporate transparency via an environmental or sustainability report is that stakeholder relations are strengthened. Confidence and trust between the two parties are improved when organizations include stakeholders in the reporting process by actively engaging with them. Stakeholder dialogue is increasingly used by large companies to help identify the key issues that are of concern to their stakeholders. Appropriate issues should then be addressed in the environmental report.

Increased competitive advantage

An organization that demonstrates full responsibility for its environmental impacts and then reports on them benefits from gaining a competitive edge over its peers in the same sector that are not as open and transparent about such issues. Environmental reporting may provide competitive advantage in capital, labour, supplier and customer markets.

Improved access to lists of 'preferred suppliers'

Corporate environmental stewardship now includes consideration of upstream processes. Suppliers that share the same high environmental values as buyers with green procurement policies, and that can openly report on all aspects of their performance, thus giving a more complete and transparent view of the organization's managerial strategy and operations, are more likely to achieve 'preferred supplier' status.

Reduced corporate risk

In the reporting cycle it is now common to identify the areas of environmental and social risk, which previously went unnoticed. By actively lowering these corporate risks, compliance will increase while potential liabilities will decrease, thereby reducing financing costs and, possibly, broadening the range of investors.

Assistance with investment analysis

If a company accounts for all its impacts and performance measures (economic, environmental and social), investors will obtain a clearer picture of its true health. Socially responsible investment, where companies are screened prior to investment, using social and environmental criteria, is growing exponentially. Environmental and sustainability reports aid analysis and, for some funds, reporting is a requirement.

Stakeholders and their information needs

Whereas published financial data are assumed to be important primarily to shareholders, lenders and potential investors in enabling them to make economic decisions relating to the reporting entity, with environmental and sustainability reporting there is no such certainty, as there is potentially a much wider audience for environmental, social and economic data.

For example, NGOs need to be shown that secured assets are not impaired in any way; local communities may require site-specific data relating to emission, waste policies and wider community issues; and shareholders and financial analysts will need assurance that poor environmental management will not translate into financial risk. Other stakeholders include customers that may have strict environment and social procurement policies and employees who need assurance on health and safety grounds and assurance that they are working for a responsible and accountable employer.

Many reporters make a considerable effort to identify who their primary stakeholders are and to establish an ongoing dialogue with them to ensure that the published reports meet their needs. A comprehensive stakeholder survey is an essential prerequisite for publishing a first environmental or sustainability report. Thereafter, companies may set up stakeholder panels or focus groups to maintain the process of dialogue and feedback. Feedback forms are usually included in published reports, and web-based reports normally incorporate a mechanism for delivering feedback through the website itself.

The Global Reporting Initiative

The Global Reporting Initiative (GRI) was originally established as a voluntary cooperative initiative in late 1997 with the objective of developing a set of reporting guidelines dealing with the economic, environmental and social consequences of organizational activity. The international steering committee that led the initiative brought together the world's leading reporting experts and organizations, including ACCA. The first set of formal 'sustainability reporting' guidelines was published in June 2000.

The growth in support for the objectives of the GRI has been wide-ranging. Apart from around 450 organizations across 45 countries that currently use the GRI in whole or in part as a basis for developing their own corporate sustainability reports, the GRI has received widespread support at the governmental and institutional level as a tool that has the potential to provide the transparency and accountability increasingly being demanded of multinational companies by their stakeholders.

The GRI's mode of working is based around a number of principles or qualities that provide the underpinning legitimacy for its recommendations. The GRI is non-aligned and multi-stakeholder in structure and governance. The organizational model is inclusive and aspires to be global in outreach. Governance and working methods are transparent. Its guidelines are voluntary, not mandatory, and are dynamic in that they are constantly being tested, reviewed and upgraded. The first board of directors was selected in 2003, and Roger Adams, Executive Director – Technical, ACCA, was successfully nominated. The board of directors has the ultimate fiduciary, financial and legal responsibility for the GRI, and exercises final decision-making authority on revisions to the guidelines, technical work and organizational strategy.

The GRI 2002 Guidelines

The second, expanded version of the GRI reporting guidelines was issued in 2002. The 2002 Guidelines represent a significant step forward for sustainability reporting, containing as they do an improved set of environmental indicators alongside much-expanded sets of social and economic performance indicators. The 2002 Guidelines are divided into four parts:

■ *Part A: Using the Guidelines.* An informative overview of the Guidelines, including a description of what they are, who should use them and how to prepare a report using them.

■ *Part B: Reporting principles.* A description of each principle and how it is organized.

■ *Part C: Report content.* A description of the content of a GRI report. A GRI report consists of 'Vision and strategy', 'Profile', 'Governance structure and management systems', 'GRI content index' and 'Performance (economic, environmental, social) indicators'.

■ *Part D: Glossary and annexes.* A number of annexes are included on issues such as credibility and assurance, and incremental application, together with a glossary.

It should be stressed that the GRI Guidelines can be used and implemented on an incremental basis. The GRI acknowledges that some organizations, particularly smaller ones and first-time reporters, may be able to adopt only part of the Guidelines in the first instance. It is hoped, however, that reporters will increase the quantity and quality of their reporting over time.

The GRI in the future

The GRI has now embarked on creating a 'family' of GRI-related documents. The elements of this family are:

1. The core guidelines: the foundation document upon which all other GRI documents are based. These are due to be updated in 2006.
2. Sector-specific supplements providing additional guidance for specific sectors, which address issues pertinent to those industries. Current sector reports being developed include mining and metals, financial services, and public sector guidelines.
3. Measurement/technical protocols, each one addressing a specific set of indicators and providing technical guidance on their measurement.
4. Issues papers, which are issue-specific supplements to provide additional models for organizing the information.

For further information on the GRI and to download the GRI 2002 Guidelines, please visit www.globalreporting.org.

Components of a sustainability report

Many environmental reporting guidelines have evolved over the past decade to provide organizations with a framework of what to include in an environmental report. More recently, the GRI has provided guidance on what to include in a sustainability report. The following sections highlight the main components of an ideal sustainability report.

CEO's statement

A statement from the CEO or the chair of the board of directors helps to demonstrate the degree of commitment to, and support for, corporate accountability. Statements should refer to the organization's policies and should also make reference to achievements and low points of the year, issues and challenges that lie ahead for the company, and its future sustainability strategy.

Organizational profile

The organizational profile is an overview of the organization in terms of its size, structure and spread of activities, as represented, for example, by turnover and number of operational sites and employees and the markets and market segments served. The key interactions with the physical environment with regard to the company's products or services and operations should be included. Any related health and safety information can also be included in the organizational profile.

Scope

A number of report 'boundaries' should be stated to better inform users of the report – for example:

- What part of the organization is included – all the sites or just headquarters? Global or national operations? Are subsidiaries and joint ventures included?
- What is the scope of content – social, environmental and/or economic?
- What period of time does the report cover?

Key impacts

All businesses have an impact on society and the environment, but the extent of this impact depends on many factors, including the size, sector and location of the business. The significant impacts should be clearly explained so that readers can understand the burden of the business. Disclosures under this heading will be strongly influenced by the feedback obtained from organizational stakeholders as to what they consider to be the main impacts and the areas on which they request performance disclosures.

Governance

The 2002 GRI Sustainability Reporting Guidelines have a 'Governance and management systems' section that should help organizations address this important sustainability issue in future reports. Issues that should be addressed include the governance structure (such as committees and their responsibilities) and the organizational structure of individuals responsible for day-to-day implementation of strategy and policy.

Sustainability-related policies

A public commitment to pursue particular goals and objectives in terms of managing, measuring and reporting environmental, social and/or economic performance against specific targets should be made.

Management systems and procedures

The provision of reliable performance information is impossible without adequate information systems having been established in the first instance. This section typically describes the environmental and related other management systems in place, including staff contact details and members of the board who are responsible for environmental management training programmes and related educational activities for staff, any external accreditation achieved (eg ISO 14000/EMS) and key managerial responsibilities for the various aspects of the system.

Stakeholder engagement

All organizations' reports should state who the report is intended for, and should disclose who the company's stakeholders are in general. Reports should describe their stakeholder consultation and dialogue processes and explain how any stakeholder feedback has been used and how stakeholders are involved in the reporting process.

Performance and compliance

Detailed performance data form the central feature of the best reports. Such data comprehensively illustrate success (or failure) in making progress towards achieving the stated targets. This section can include information on physical data, prosecutions and complaints, and financial data. Stakeholder feedback is an excellent pointer as to which specific performance indicators will be of most interest to external parties.

Targets and achievements

Target setting helps to demonstrate an organization's commitment to improve its performance continually. Feedback on achievements for previously set targets can demonstrate the positive strides the company has made towards meeting its overall objectives. A comprehensive set of targets should cover all key environmental, social and economic issues faced.

Independent verification statement

Most organizations have realized that, without independent assurance, their report will have little standing with any external audience. Verification statements cover systems compliance issues and provide assurance as to the completeness of the report. The best verification statements also report on the acceptability performance and offer recommendations for systems improvement and reporting practice. Factors the verifier should bear in mind include:

- remit and scope;
- indication of site visits and site-specific testing;
- interpretation of data or performance reported;
- identification of any data or information omitted that could or should have been included;
- independent comment on corporate targets set and impacts identified;
- shortcomings and recommendations.

2

Core issues in business management

A new framework for business: legal overview

James Samuel, Simmons & Simmons

There is a widely held view that the expanding number and complexity of legal requirements, particularly in the areas of environmental and health and safety law, is putting an intolerable burden on industry, in particular SMEs. Although, with a few exceptions, much of the new legislation has been preceded by extensive discussion and consultation and so should not take industry entirely by surprise, there has needed to be an increase in the amount of environmental, health and safety legislation in order to comply with European obligations and to deliver UK policy objectives. It is essential to have an 'early warning system' to detect changes in law and policy that will have a significant effect on a business – this can be a feature of environmental management systems.

There is also a concern that industry is being exposed to some heavy-handed enforcement by environmental and health and safety regulators. Whilst it is fair to say that one measure of a regulator's success can be its enforcement statistics, the suggestion that prosecutions are commenced or enforcement notices issued inappropriately is difficult to substantiate. There is no doubt, however, that the days when it was cheaper to 'pay the fine' than comply with a legislative requirement are at an end. Public expectations and government policy fully support higher fines for prosecutions for environment and health and safety offences.

Personal liability of directors and officers has been a feature of environment, health and safety law for many years. However, there has been an increasing focus on this issue and a sense that the directors of companies must ensure that they are better aware of the situation within their own organization that relates to environment and health and safety performance. Whilst, to date, there have been relatively few custodial sentences imposed on company directors, the issue is a real one. The much-publicized draft Corporate Manslaughter Bill is intended to update existing laws on corporate killing by providing a more effective sanction for holding companies and other organizations to account when gross negligence in their senior management has had fatal consequences. This legislation would not introduce new standards but reinforce the need for organizations to meet their existing health and safety obligations.

Economic instruments, including those establishing and implementing 'green taxes' designed to deliver environmental improvements by making it more costly not to comply, can impose additional costs on business as well as being quite complicated to comply with. For example, the steps to be taken to obtain an exemption from the payment of landfill tax for remediation of contaminated land contain many pitfalls.

SUSTAINABLE INFRASTRUCTURE INVESTMENT OPTIONS FOR PENSION FUNDS

Thomas S. Murley

Director, Energy Investments, HgCapital, London

Introduction

Companies seeking to reach sustainability goals frequently overlook investing their pension funds in sustainable activities. Naturally, the focus is on reducing pollution, using recycled materials, energy efficiency and other immediate and direct actions to enhance sustainability. Over the last decade, maturing sustainable technologies such as wind energy, coupled with the emergence of experienced professional investment managers, now allow company pension fund trustees to further sustainable goals whilst earning attractive investments returns.

There are several sustainable investment options for pension funds, including:

- Listed clean energy and socially responsible investment (SRI) funds that invest in listed companies that (i) pursue sustainable activities such as British Petroleum and General Electric, (ii) manufacturers of clean energy or pollution control technologies, such as wind turbines and (iii) owners and operators of clean technologies such as wind farms and biofuel facilities.

- "Clean Tech" funds, which are typically venture capital funds that invest in emerging companies and technologies in energy, pollution control, waste management.

- Carbon funds, which invest in tradable carbon emissions credits created by the Kyoto Protocol on climate change.

- Private infrastructure funds that invest in operating renewable energy projects such as wind farms, biofuel facilities and solar energy projects.

This paper focuses on the last category, private infrastructure funds.

Pension Fund Types

There are two basic Pension funds, defined benefit or final salary plans, and defined contribution plans. In defined benefit plans, employees are guaranteed a fixed pension amount for life, usually based on salary at retirement. This is funded by company and employee contributions, and investment decisions are made by trustees who seek investments to meet the fixed obligations.

In defined contribution schemes, employee and employer contributions are invested in an account personal to the employee. Employees have a range of investment options, usually listed funds, depending on their risk appetite. The contributions and any investment returns (or losses) are paid over the employee at retirement.

Broadly speaking, only listed investment options are appropriate or available to defined contribution plans, whilst all listed and unlisted options may be pursued by defined benefit plans.

Alternative Investments

Historically, pension funds invested in listed equities, corporate and government bonds, and sometimes real estate. Since the 1980's pension funds (especially defined benefit plans) have dramatically increased their exposure to "alternative investments", including private equity, hedge funds and infrastructure. The following table shows the growth in US and European private equity (buyout and venture funds) from 1990 through 2005.

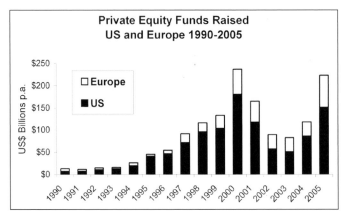

Source: Price Waterhouse Coopers, Venture Economics, Dow Jones, European Venture Capital Journal

There are many reasons for this asset allocation shift: inability to meet pension fund obligations from traditional investments; low interest rates, which reduce income from fixed income investments; erratic listed equity returns and forecast returns at the historic 8% mean; and superior investment performance from the alternative assets. The primary drivers, however, remain the potential for higher returns from alternatives and fund managers' proven ability to deliver those returns.

Infrastructure Investments

Infrastructure investment also grew since the 1980s. The first infrastructure funds were established in the US for power generation followed by Australian funds for toll roads and airports. Today, infrastructure investments are common, and capital flows are increasing. From 1990 to 2002, approximately $30 billion was invested in infrastructure funds. Since 2002, a further $20 billion has been raised for investments in power generation, roads, airports, ports, pipelines, refineries, hospitals and waste facilities.[1] The recent growth over the prior 12 years is due to a maturing of the infrastructure investment sector, allowing investors to benchmark infrastructure returns against other investment options. What is the attraction of infrastructure assets?

Infrastructure assets generally combine low risk and high cash flow relative to other investments. Think of a gas pipeline. It is simple to operate and maintain; it has a 30 to 40 year life, and its customers are large, credit worthy energy companies who enter long-term contracts to lease pipeline space. After operating and finance expenses, such assets pay regular dividends, which equal and often exceed returns from bonds and other listed investments. Further, until the very latest years of their lives they tend to hold their capital value. Because the assets are long lived and will generate cash for their entire lives, they fit well with pension funds, who seek to match investment opportunities with their long-term liabilities to pensioners.

The traditional attributes of infrastructure investments which make them attractive to long-term investors include:

- *Limited competition; predictable or guaranteed revenues*. Think of the pipeline again. Because of permitting restrictions and high costs, it is unlikely that a pipeline will be built to compete with an existing pipeline. Therefore, many infrastructure assets have a stable market base, which allows predictable revenues. Others, such as power plants, pipelines and waste facilities have long-term revenue contracts (5-25 years) or benefit from government-set tariffs, which assure long-term income.

- *Predictable costs*. Most infrastructure assets use proven technologies, and there is sufficient history to accurately forecast normal operating costs and capital expenditures. In many cases, a large portion of the operating

[1] Source: HgCapital Research

costs are borne by equipment suppliers through long-term maintenance and repair contracts. Similarly, most new infrastructure assets are constructed under fixed price contracts in which the contractor assumes the costs and risks of delay and cost overruns.

- *Favourable regulatory environment.* Governments are increasingly turning to the private sector to build, operate and finance infrastructure assets to conserve government finances for social investments such as pensions, healthcare, education and security. The private sector has demonstrated that it can manage and operate infrastructure projects more efficiently than government. Thus, there is an extremely favourable regulatory environment to encourage private investment. The UK Private Finance Initiative and the support mechanisms and tax breaks for renewable energy and renewable fuels are examples.

- *Favourable inflation correlation.* For most infrastructure assets, their long-term revenue contracts are linked to inflation. Whilst costs too are also linked to inflation, because they represent less than 100% of revenues, returns tend to increase as inflation increases, thus allowing infrastructure investments to often outperform in inflationary environments.

- *Long-term debt.* Because of their stable nature, infrastructure assets are able to attract long-term debt. 12-15 years are the most common tenors, but tenors of up to 20-25 years are available for certain assets such as pipelines and hospitals. The interest rate risk is managed through swaps and other interest rate protection scheme which largely or fully insulate the projects from interest rate increases.

- *Increasing Liquidity.* When infrastructure investing began in the late 1980s and early 1990s, there were questions about the market for liquidating these investments. In recent years, a number of active buyers and secondary markets have emerged for infrastructure asset, providing the necessary liquidity.

Investing in Renewable and Sustainable Infrastructure

Since 1995, there has been substantial growth in sustainable infrastructure projects, primarily in the areas of renewable power generation, biofuels and waste-to-energy. This growth has accelerated in recent years based on the following fundamentals:

- Improvements in technologies that allow renewable energies to compete with conventional sources.

- Concerns over high oil and gas prices.

- Concerns about energy security/import levels.

- The need to reduce carbon dioxide emissions to stem global warming.

For example, since 1995 European wind farm installations have grown at an annual compounded rate of over 30%.[2] The pace of investment is not expected to abate, and many expect it to accelerate. Sustainable infrastructure is capital intensive, requiring over €10-12 billion per year in capital expenditure through 2010 in Western Europe alone. This creates an annual equity market of over €2 billion per year.[3]

In Europe, these facilities have all the attributes of infrastructure investments in general:

- *Revenue visibility and inflation correlation.* Renewable power generation, such as wind, solar and waste-to-energy enjoy tariffs or contracts to sell power generated for 12-20 years. Most often these are linked to inflation and the buyers are investment grade utilities. For biofuels, government mandates for an increasing percentage of bio input in diesel fuels assures a market with major oil suppliers.

- *Proven technologies and operating costs.* There are now over 75,000 wind turbines operating globally. Biofuel production plants have been operating in the US and Brazil for nearly a decade. As a result of this experience, long-term operating costs are known, and thus long-term profit margins and cash flows to investors are predictable. In the case of wind, the manufacturers guaranty fixed operating costs up to 15 years.

- *Favourable regulation.* Since 1990, European countries have pursued strong national renewable energy policies. In 2001 the EU adopted a renewable energy directive, under which EU members agreed to source 12.5% of electricity from renewable resources by 2010. It is a key leg in achieving Europe's obligations under the Kyoto Protocol to reduce greenhouse gas emissions to 8% below 1990 levels. To implement the directive, countries

[2] Source: BTM Consult
[3] Source: HgCapital Research, BTM Consult.

have enacted a variety of support measures, ranging from streamlined permitting and tax breaks to guaranteed long-term revenue arrangements. In 2003 an EU directive set a 5.75% biofuels target by 2010.

- *Long-term debt finance.* There is an active and liquid bank finance market for renewable energy assets in Europe, with tenors extending to 20 years.

- *Liquidity.* Since 2002, a substantial secondary market has arisen for operating renewable energy assets. They buyers include utilities, listed funds and private equity funds. This coincides with the increased liquidity in infrastructure assets in general.

Conclusion

Investments in sustainable infrastructure assets can provide pension funds with attractive, risk-adjusted returns. The long duration of the asset makes them an excellent match for long-term pension liabilities. With strong sector fundamentals, strong cash generation, increasing liquidity, and a number of experienced investment experts now focused on the market, it is an investment option that pension fund trustees should consider to enhance returns and portfolio diversification.

Risk management

Greg Pritchard, CPA Audit

The balance between risk and reward is the very essence of business; it is necessary to take risks in order to generate returns. There is, however, a difference between risks taken as a result of careful judgement and those taken unwittingly or unknowingly. In today's world of increasing complexity and uncertainty, businesses must manage risk more rigorously than ever before.

Thus, risk management should be a key feature of any successful business, and carrying out a thorough risk assessment is the starting point. Completion of such an assessment typically adopts the following process:

- *Step 1*. Identify the risk drivers for each category of risk, including business strategy, market, political and economic environment, customers, products and services, operations and distribution, suppliers, credit and financial soundness, management and staff. This activity is usually carried out in a workshop, brain-storming or focus group setting.
- *Step 2*. Allocate a probability of the risks identified arising. This is a subjective assessment and can be in the form of a simple high, medium, low categorization. Alternatively, a more sophisticated approach could be adopted by allocating time-frames such as:
  - rare occurrence: less than once every 10 years;
  - unlikely occurrence: once every 5–10 years; and so on.
- *Step 3*. Assess the business exposure, such as loss of a customer, damage to reputation or a financial penalty, in the event of each risk arising.

■ *Step 4.* Assess the degree of impact resulting from the business exposure. Again, this can be a subjective assessment in the simple form of high, medium, low, or a more sophisticated approach can be taken based on likely monetary losses, such as:
  – insignificant: loss less than £10 million;
  – minor: loss between £10 million and £25 million; and so on.

With the risk assessment complete, the business will know with some degree of certainty what risks it faces, how likely they are to arise and the likely impact on the business in the event that they do arise. Naturally, the risk assessment should be monitored and reviewed on a regular basis in case the risk profile of the business changes.

Not surprisingly, the next step is to identify the control mechanisms in place to prevent the risks arising or to mitigate their effects. Here the focus should be on those risks that are more likely to arise and have a significant detrimental impact on the business when they do arise; these are the areas where the most robust internal controls are required.

The nature and extent of the systems and controls that a business will need to maintain will depend upon a variety of factors, including:

■ the nature, scale and complexity of its business;
■ the diversity of its operations;
■ the volume and size of its transactions;
■ the degree of risk associated with each area of its operations.

Typical control mechanisms include supervision, monitoring and review, reconciliations, segregation of duties, exception reporting, disaster recovery and business continuity planning, physical security, documentation, insurance and, of course, internal audit. Other constituents of the risk management toolkit include risk committees and stress and scenario testing. To be truly effective, a company's internal control system should:

■ be embedded within its operations and not treated as a separate exercise;
■ be able to respond to changing risks within and outside the company;
■ enable the company to apply it in an appropriate manner related to its risks.

Here, factors to consider include:

■ the nature and extent of the risks facing the company;
■ the extent and categories of risk that it is regarded as acceptable for the company to bear;
■ the likelihood of the risks concerned materializing;
■ the company's ability to reduce the incidence and impact on the business of risks that do materialize;
■ the costs of operating controls relative to the benefit obtained from managing the risks.

Table 2.2.1 Format for recording and displaying the results of a risk assessment

Category of Risk	Risk Driver	Probability	Exposure	Impact	Control Mechanism	Audit Test
Staff	Loss of key individuals	Medium	Loss of knowledge, expertise and commercial contacts	Low to high depending on business area	Cross-training and spreading client relationships Procedures manuals, work schedules and other documentation, particularly relating to IT systems Provisions of attractive career opportunities and competitive compensation packages	Review results of employee skills audit and client relationship management arrangements Review procedures manuals, work schedules, IT system documentation etc for completeness Compare remuneration packages against comparable industry benchmark data
	Insufficient segregation of duties	Low	Potential for fraud or hiding mistakes resulting in loss to the company	Medium	Exception reporting from IT systems Management review Independent confirmation and/or reconciliation with third parties	

Table 2.2.1 Format for recording and displaying the results of a risk assessment (*continued*)

Category of Risk	Risk Driver	Probability	Exposure	Impact	Control Mechanism	Audit Test
	Critical systems not supported when staff are absent	Low to high depending on business area	Interruption of normal business cycle	High	Cross-training Use of subcontractors where no suitable internal resource exists	Review results of employee skills audit Review procedure for selecting, and assessing the competence of, subcontractors
	Normal procedures not carried out and normal controls not applied when staff are absent	Low	Potential for error or fraud increases Breach of client investment guidelines	Medium	System controls and warnings and other manual procedures Cross-training and absence cover	
	Poor-quality or inexperienced staff deliver inadequate client service and/or provide inadequate advice	Low	Client dissatisfaction Damage to reputation Regulatory concern	High	Tight recruitment procedures to ensure only suitably qualified individuals are employed Staff training and professional development	

Risk area	Risk	Likelihood	Consequence	Impact	Controls
Systems	Loss or corruption of data	Low	Interruption of normal business cycle	High	Daily back-up procedure; Anti-virus software
	System failure	Low	Inability to conduct business	High	Presence of emergency site; Emergency power supply
	Confidential data strays into the public domain	Low	Client dissatisfaction; Damage to reputation; Regulatory concern	Low	Use of firewall to protect internet connection; Systems protected by passwords; Attempt to penetrate the firewall
Compliance and regulation	Failure to comply with regulations	Low	Fines, loss of licences	High	Regular review of activities by Compliance Officer
	Loss of Compliance Officer	Low	Increased risk of non-compliance and breach of regulations due to inadequate supervision	Medium	Use of other members of staff (with appropriate experience) or external consultants
Health and safety	Accidents to personnel	Low	Temporary loss of personnel; Claims for compensation	Low	See staff section above; Periodic checks conducted by Health and Safety Officer; Insurance

Table 2.2.1 Format for recording and displaying the results of a risk assessment (*continued*)

Category of Risk	Risk Driver	Probability	Exposure	Impact	Control Mechanism	Audit Test
Security	Unauthorized intrusion	Low	Physical attacks on personnel Loss of equipment Confidential	Low	Insurance Door entry security system Nightwatchman Data back-ups	
Operational and delivery	Incorrect order execution	Low	Company assumes an unintentional proprietary position Company required to compensate client(s) for profits that would have arisen on the correct trade or losses incurred on the incorrect trade	Medium	Order read back to client Fill confirmed to client Transaction note sent to client	

Risk		Consequence		Controls
Incorrect recording of trades	Low	Company assumes an unintentional proprietary position Unknown open positions give rise to losses for which the company will eventually have to provide compensation	Medium	Back-office reconciliations to order confirmations Transaction note sent to client
Late settlement of futures contracts which go to delivery	Low	Fines imposed by the London Clearing House Clients dissatisfied	Medium	Exception report of trades approaching delivery sent to dealing desk and followed up by back office
Late or incorrect payment instructions when funds are remitted to clients or counterparties	Low	Possible financial loss to the company	Medium	Standard settlement payments are checked against a list daily; US$ payments require sign-off by one authorized signatory, GB£ payments require sign-off by two authorized signatories

Table 2.2.1 Format for recording and displaying the results of a risk assessment (*continued*)

Category of Risk	Risk Driver	Probability	Exposure	Impact	Control Mechanism	Audit Test
					All other payments are confirmed by telephone	
Counter-party and credit	Failure of counterparty	Low	The cost of settling open foreign exchange contracts and open futures contracts would accrue to the company Loss of cash deposits lodged with counterparty as margin to collateralize trading lines	Low	Trade only with approved counterparties Periodic review of financial standing of counterparties	

Category	Risk	Likelihood	Impact	Rating	Controls	Audit tests
	Volatile market conditions result in exceptional losses that clients are unable or unwilling to cover	Medium	Client losses accrue to company	Medium	Periodic review of client creditworthiness; Management of the size of positions in relation to individual limits and in relation to the size of the overall market; Awareness of events likely to cause market volatility and associated contingency planning; Margin call management	Review documentation relating to recent client creditworthiness checks for high-value positions in volatile commodities; Review the size of positions in relation to individual limits and the size of the overall market; Review contingency plans for events currently likely to cause market volatility; Review recent margin call activity, noting the speed with which clients respond
Market and performance	Poor advice given to advisory and discretionary clients	Low	Damage to reputation affecting client retention and new business development	Medium	Selection procedures for recruiting dealers who are required to pass FSA exams; Client agreements absolve responsibility for bad advice	

A convenient tabular format for recording and displaying the results of the risk assessment process is shown in Table 2.2.1.

If the business has an internal audit department, it should use the risk assessment to direct the business's resources in order to evaluate whether an adequate level of internal control exists to reduce business risks to an acceptable level. Thus, internal audit resource should be focused on reviewing and testing the effectiveness of those internal controls in place to prevent, mitigate, minimize or transfer risk caused by events that have a high to medium probability of occurrence and give rise to a correspondingly high to medium detrimental impact. Naturally, internal control mechanisms should be refined or created where these are found to be ineffective or missing. Used in this way, internal audit will become a valuable tool for corporate boards in their endeavours to achieve business objectives efficiently and objectively by maintaining and improving internal controls commensurate with business risk. Such an approach also constitutes best practice with regard to corporate governance.

CPA Audit provides professional advice to the financial services sector in the areas of:

- regulatory compliance;
- risk management;
- internal audit;
- corporate governance.

It also provides a range of consultancy and support services, including executive search, company secretarial services, fund administration and the preparation of FSA financial returns. For more details, please go to http://www.cpaaudit.co.uk.

Defined in this way, the idea of supplier diversity clearly fits well with current debates and policy preferences in the UK. For example:

■ It can be seen as an integral part of the corporate social responsibility (CSR) agenda.
■ It sits alongside current government policies to promote equal opportunities, greater social inclusion and good race relations.
■ It helps to develop the approach of 'Think small first' in respect of supply chain relationships being developed in the public sector.
■ It can contribute to the long-standing practice of encouraging local economic development through the use of the procurement process.

As the above points illustrate, the environment in which modern firms operate requires them to think beyond the idea of business as a purely economic institution that exists for the sole purpose of creating value for its owners. Both government and the public are increasingly aware that the business community has a key part to play in achieving broader social as well as economic goals. In procurement, buying in a socially responsible way ensures that non-economic criteria are brought into the equation – these can be ethical factors, sustainability criteria or environmental elements. By purchasing in this way, the procurement professional is contributing towards achieving a form of positive social change desired by society.

The legislative framework

In the United States, a legislative framework provides encouragement and support in the promotion of greater civil rights. In the US public sector, for example, public sector bodies are legally required to buy 25 per cent of their goods and services from 'diverse' suppliers. Under the US National Minority Supplier Development Council (NMSDC), a minority business is defined as one that is 51 per cent or more owned and controlled by members of certain designated minority groups, including racial and ethnic minorities, women, the disabled, war veterans, gays or lesbians.

In the UK and Europe there is no such legislative framework currently in existence. Rather than promoting equality of 'outcome', the focus in the UK is on 'equal treatment'. The Race Relations Act 2002 gives public authorities a statutory duty to promote racial equality and requires them to prevent unlawful discrimination in areas such as service delivery and employment practice (www.cre.gov.uk). Similar competition policies exist in the EU. These existing laws in both the UK and the EU could be said to limit severely the scope for organizations to give preference to targeted groups of potential suppliers.

However, there is no denying that discrimination and social exclusion are two topics high on the agenda at present, and further legislation seems likely to help outlaw discriminatory practice based on race and ethnicity. In addition, future European procurement legislation is currently being reviewed that may widen the scope to allow public procurement to achieve greater equality of opportunity. This would therefore mean that in the future companies with a supplier diversity programme could be at a competitive advantage when bidding for public contracts in the EU.

Supplier diversity[1]

The Chartered Institute of Purchasing and Supply (CIPS)

Understanding supplier diversity

'Diversity' refers to the idea of variety, a central feature of the world that we and other species inhabit. In business we see this variety manifest itself in many ways. Owing to the nature of today's economy, there are organizations of different shapes and sizes serving different sectors with different needs. Businesses acquire finance and other resources from different sources. Diversity is a way of life – with most workforces consisting of individuals of differing age, racial and ethnic background, sexual orientation, religion and so on. This diversity is both natural and enriching: it provides opportunities and experiences that would be missing from a world where everything was totally homogeneous.

Supplier diversity as a concept can be explained as: 'Initiatives that aim to increase the number of diverse (eg ethnic-minority owned, women-owned) businesses that supply goods and services to both public and private sector organizations, either directly or as part of a wider emphasis on smaller enterprises in general.'[2]

This concept centres on offering under-represented businesses the same opportunities to compete for the supply of goods and services as other qualified suppliers. From the purchasers' point of view, supplier diversity initiatives are not seeking to discriminate positively in favour of certain types of business (eg based on size or the gender or ethnicity of the owner) but rather to create a 'level playing field' allowing an equal chance to all firms of achieving the custom.

Making good business sense of supplier diversity

Race for Opportunity (part of Business in the Community) defines 'supplier diversity' as follows: 'Supplier diversity refers to initiatives that aim to increase the number of ethnic minority-owned businesses that supply goods and services to both public and private sector organizations. It promotes supplier participation reflective of the diverse business community.'[3] It states: 'The business case for supplier diversity initiatives is based on the premise that there are potential economic benefits to large organizations from purchasing locally. The idea is that there are local businesses that can provide goods and services to major private purchasers at better value and with greater efficiency.'[4]

Although supplier diversity policies can operate on a stand-alone basis, often they form part of an organization's approach to, or policy on, CSR. There is great debate about what drives an organization to adopt more socially responsible practices – whether it's legislation, stakeholder pressure or feeling they want to do it. However, it is now more commonly recognized that socially responsible behaviour in business is good practice, not least because it can reduce the risk of damage to an organization's reputation in the media, the marketplace and broader society.

New opportunities

Many ethnic minority businesses buy and sell within their own community, with businesses owned by people from the same ethnic group. This concentration of activity may offer a clear focus for business support activity. However, it can also limit the potential growth among small businesses and can create vulnerability resulting from over-dependence on specific markets.[5] But for organizations outside of those communities there is the potential to discover an untapped source of both suppliers and sales opportunities.

The 2012 London Olympics presents both a massive challenge and an opportunity for SMEs and ethnic minority businesses. This project is enormous and will provide abundant opportunities for suppliers to work with the Olympic Delivery Authority (ODA). Tessa Jowell, Culture Secretary, speaking at a business summit in early 2006, said: 'The government will be spending £3 billion on infrastructure for the games and we want that money to work to the benefit of our economy. This doesn't mean a "Buy British" campaign, but we want to ensure public money is recycled into the British economy' – while acting within European law. David Higgins, the chief executive of the ODA, which is responsible for delivering the infrastructure of the games, said that the goal was for procurement to promote best practice in areas including ethical sourcing, supply chain management and supplier diversity.

Increased commitment and flexibility

For SMEs and ethnic minority businesses, orders from large corporate bodies could represent a significant share of their turnover, therefore encouraging greater commitment and high levels of service. Having a broader supply base can also help an organization by offering greater flexibility in its procurement decisions and can help provide additional supply chain security in the event of a disruption.

Sources of innovation and competitiveness

Sourcing products and services from ethnic minority businesses can also bring about value and innovation to the supply base. Diversity amongst suppliers opens up possibilities of using innovative and/or cost-effective solutions that might help to provide an organization with a strategic advantage either through differentiation or through cost leadership.

Mirroring the customer base

As globalization takes a firmer hold, organizations are finding that their customer base is also more diverse. Using ethnic minority businesses to form part of a supplier base may mean that organizations can mirror their suppliers and their customers better. For organizations such as BT, engaging with suppliers that reflect their changing customer demographics is seen as a business imperative and one that helps to 'embed' their organizations within the different ethnic communities that buy their products and services.

The business case

Because our customers are so diverse, the issue of diversity is commercially important to us and built into our business objectives. We must understand and align ourselves with our customers if we are to provide a truly world-class service.

Supplier diversity

During the 2005 financial year, we participated in the European Supplier Diversity Programme. This looks at how diversity can be encouraged in supply chains. We held a workshop to understand the issues that diverse suppliers may encounter when competing for business with big companies.

We sent The Way We Work booklet to current suppliers to reinforce how we value diversity in the workforce and how we expect our suppliers to reflect this when working with BT.

(Taken from www.btplc.com)

Engaging on a local level

Ethnic minority businesses can be a critical element of the ethnic community and often the wider local economy. They can provide an important source of employment and business opportunities within the ethnic community and help to stimulate local economic and social development and growth. By using ethnic minority suppliers, larger organizations can help improve the economic and social outlook of local communities, thereby creating greater opportunities to supply goods and services to local individuals and organizations by boosting local purchasing power.

Developing an organization's resource base

It is often said that organizations that engage in socially responsible practices tend to enhance their resource base by creating goodwill in the community and by improving their reputation with key stakeholder groups, including customers and employees. What these groups think about an organization can be crucial in its commercial performance. Survey evidence suggests that a favourable reputation can have an important impact on recruitment and retention and is likely to feed through to staff morale, loyalty and productivity.

An additional consequence of this is that, by engaging in socially responsible procurement, organizations can reduce the risk of a negative response by important organizational stakeholders. It can also help to put the organization ahead of any change in government regulations, which could help to reduce the future costs of compliance.

For procurement professionals, establishing a supplier diversity programme should not be seen as simply a public relations exercise; potentially it can also provide opportunities to add real value to the organization on both the demand and the supply side. Engaging in behaviour that develops closer links with minority suppliers promises a range of intangible benefits for the organization and can help to enhance its standing in the wider community.

Challenging the issues

The benefits identified make the prospect of a supplier diversity programme an attractive one, but achieving diversity in the supply chain can encounter some contentious issues.

Organizational change of any kind needs to have senior management buy-in. Achieving that support can often present a significant challenge, particularly within the context of the existing structure of corporate governance. In many large organizations, procurement is still not a boardroom agenda item. This lack of knowledge and understanding can represent a substantial barrier to the introduction of a supplier diversity programme.

Opposition may also be felt from other areas of the organization, whether it's internal in terms of employees or from an external source such as customers. There may be a misunderstanding amongst customers about the nature of, or reasons for, greater supplier diversity. Existing suppliers may also feel threatened by this new development and may feel that preferential treatment is being given to one group of bidders.

Alignment and coordination

Incorporating a supplier diversity programme into an existing set of corporate policies, processes and procedures raises a number of strategic and operational questions. Does the new initiative contribute to the organization's current strategic position? Will it add value to the procurement process, and is it consistent with the existing procurement strategy? To what extent will it give rise to difficulties in coordinating the objectives and activities of members of the supply chain both internally and externally? These and other issues of alignment and coordination require careful consideration prior to the introduction of a supplier diversity programme.

Supplier Development East Midlands (SDEM)

Managed by the Centre for Research in Ethnic Minority Entrepreneurship (CREME) at De Montfort University, Leicester, the SDEM programme attempts to bring corporate Britain and ethnic minority businesses together in order to conduct meaningful business. The programme has established a unique case of knowledge transfer via a partnering initiative with the National Minority Supplier Development Council (NMSDC), which is helping SDEM in recruiting US multinationals that have a UK presence. Established in June 2004, SDEM is headed by a steering group of 14 large purchasing organizations from both the public and the private sector with a commitment to promote supplier diversity within their respective organizations. The programme has started developing a quality database of ethnic minority businesses across the UK, which is accessible to all its corporate members. Interaction between the corporate members and the ethnic minority businesses is achieved through a series of workshops, 'meet the buyer' events and mentoring seminars. These events provide a platform where buyers and suppliers can meet, and discuss and explore business opportunities. During the first year of its operation, a number of successes have been achieved. Two businesses have been successful in getting contracts with IBM and the Environment Agency respectively, and a number of businesses have claimed the next step in the supply chain and are negotiating contracts with a number of corporations.

Summary

Organizations seeking to establish a supplier diversity programme need to recognize that there are considerable challenges to be faced at both the strategic and the operational level. While some of these challenges lie within the organization and can start to be addressed by committing resources to programmes of education, training and development, others lie outside the direct influence and control of the organization. While there are no simple solutions to some of these problems, no barrier to change need be insurmountable given the necessary commitment to a more diverse supply base. Building this commitment is likely to be significantly facilitated if the goal of supplier diversity is championed and driven from the highest levels within the organization.

Notes

1   Large sections of this chapter have been taken from the *CIPS Guide to Supplier Diversity* as authored by Monder Ram.
2   M Ram and D Smallbone (2003) Supplier diversity initiatives and the diversification of ethnic minority businesses in the UK, *Policy Studies*, **24** (4), pp 187–204.
3   Race for Opportunity, June 2004.
4   Race for Opportunity, June 2004.
5   Ram and Smallbone (2003).

Process efficiency: legal overview

James Taylor, Simmons & Simmons

Process efficiency is not primarily a legal issue although there are numerous examples of legislation containing requirements that may necessarily involve changes to processes. For example, health and safety law requires that safe systems of work be in place. The concept of 'best available techniques' underpinning the pollution prevention control (PPC) legislation includes processes, and PPC specifically requires that the process be operated in a way that delivers improvements in energy efficiency. In addition, climate change agreements and the EU Emissions Trading Scheme will encourage industry to seek greater energy efficiency in its manufacturing processes. Changes in legislative requirements regarding the disposal of waste, in particular landfilling, have meant that many waste streams can no longer be disposed of in landfill, and much more costly options are required. Changes in process to ensure that waste streams are minimized will be a practical necessity and form the basis of the waste management hierarchy.

Funding and investment: legal overview

Julie Smith, Simmons & Simmons

The impact of sustainability issues on funding and investment decisions has been the subject of considerable research and comment. There are quite a large number of ethical or social investment funds that specialize in this area, but there are legal issues governing the structure within which they operate. For example, from July 2000 pension funds have been required to state the extent to which they take social, environmental and ethical considerations into account under the Pensions Act 1995.

The collection and provision of information relevant to investment decisions based on sustainability issues are critical. The Operating and Financial Review (OFR) Regulations make it mandatory for quoted companies to prepare an annual OFR for financial years that begin on or after 1 April 2005. The OFR must contain, 'to the extent necessary to comply with the review objective', information about environmental matters, including key performance indicators. The review objective is that the OFR provides a balanced and comprehensive analysis of the development and performance of a company's business, the position of the company at the year end, and the main trends and factors underlying the development, performance and position of the company during the financial year and in the future. An OFR must also include a description of the principal risks and uncertainties facing the company. The government's recent decision to abolish the OFR, shortly followed by a reversal of its position and announcement of a consultation on the future of the OFR, has created some uncertainty in relation to environmental reporting requirements.

Other initiatives to incorporate environmental issues into company reporting include the FTSE4Good Index Series, launched in July 2001 in response to the increasing focus on CSR by investors who wanted to measure the social, environmental and ethical performance of companies they invested in. In order to qualify for inclusion, companies must disclose how they identify, manage and report their business, social and environmental material risks to their stakeholders. Increased environmental information is also being required of companies that are seeking a stock exchange listing.

Other non-legal initiatives aimed at encouraging organizations to take an environmentally responsible stance include Business in the Community, which has 700 member companies, with a further 1,600 companies participating in programmes and campaigns. It is the longest-established organization of its kind, and its purpose is to 'inspire, challenge, engage and support business in continually improving its positive impact on society'. Membership of Business in the Community is a commitment to action and continual improvement of a company's impact on society.

International leadership is provided by bodies such as the International Finance Corporation (IFC). The IFC, which is a member of the World Bank Group, invests in private sector projects and has had a policy in place for some time that all its operations should be carried out in an environmentally and socially responsible manner. The IFC's Environment and Social Development Department is responsible for the environmental and social review, clearance and supervision of projects in a manner consistent with the requirements contained in its review procedure. In addition, to achieve better integration of environmental and social considerations within IFC operations and to ensure high performance standards, an IFC vice-president has corporate oversight of environmental and social issues and disclosure matters.

3

Transport, health, safety and employment issues

Transport: legal overview

Julie Smith, Simmons & Simmons

Transport is increasingly being recognized as a critical issue in the sustainability debate, and there are numerous initiatives designed both to change transport patterns and to reduce the impacts associated with transport.

For example, the EC directive on the use of biofuels and other renewable fuels for transport aims at promoting the replacement of diesel and petrol for transport purposes with a view to meeting climate change objectives, ensuring an environmentally friendly and secure source of supply and promoting renewable sources across Europe. The directive requires member states to set indicative targets for the years 2005 and then 2010 for the placing on the market of biofuels or other renewable fuels as a substitute for petrol or diesel used in transport. The directive suggests targets of 2 per cent by 31 December 2005 and 5.75 per cent by 2010 (calculated on the basis of energy content).

The UK has recently made provision for the introduction of a renewable transport fuel obligation modelled on the existing renewables obligation for the supply of electricity from renewable sources. The Secretary of State has a power under the Energy Act 2004 to impose an obligation on transport fuel suppliers to supply a specified amount of renewable transport fuel (broadly defined as including pure biofuels, biofuels blended with fossil fuels and any other fuel from a renewable source) to places in the UK. The government has announced that it intends to set the level of the obligation at 5 per cent by 2010. The obligation is expected to start from 1 April 2008 at the earliest.

In the UK, tax relief already exists to encourage the use of certain environmentally less damaging fuels. In 2002 a new duty rate for biodiesel was introduced at 20 pence per litre below the rate for ultra low sulphur diesel (ULSD). A similar duty differential was introduced for bioethanol on 1 January 2005. The duty incentive for LPG was decreased by the equivalent of 1 penny per litre in 2004/05 and 2005/06 and will be reduced by a further 1 penny per litre in 2006/07 to bring it to a level more commensurate with its environmental benefits.

Local authorities have statutory duties for local air quality management (LAQM) under the Environment Act 1995. They are required to carry out regular reviews and assessments of air quality in their area against standards and objectives in the national Air Quality Strategy and, where these are unlikely to be met, authorities must designate air quality management areas (AQMAs) and prepare and implement remedial action plans to tackle the problem. Monitoring undertaken by the local authorities includes nitrogen dioxide, nitrous oxides and particulates (PM_{10}) at locations near to roads throughout the UK.

The London Congestion Charging Scheme commenced charging on 17 February 2003 following the approval by the Mayor of London of orders made by Transport for London. Article 3 of the Order designates the roads within the charging area (Greater London) in respect of which charges are imposed – the zone is essentially all publicly maintainable and Crown roads within the central zone, and there are controversial proposals to extend the charging area. Annexes to the Order set out the classes of non-chargeable vehicles and reduced rate vehicles (including some alternative fuel vehicles) and the reduction for residents of the central zone. An amount (currently £8) is payable for a single-day licence if the charge is paid before 10 pm, rising to £10 between 10 pm and midnight. There are plans to extend the zone westward to cover most of Kensington and Chelsea and Westminster from 19 February 2007.

The EU Emissions Trading Directive requires the Commission to report by the end of June 2006 on whether the EU Emissions Trading Scheme should be extended to transport. In relation to aviation in particular, the Commission adopted a communication in September 2005 in which it recommends the inclusion of aviation in the Scheme. This was followed by the Council's release of supportive conclusions in December 2005 that included a request for the Commission to bring forward legislative proposals for the inclusion of aviation by the end of 2006.

Travel plans in London: good for business, good for staff, good for communities

Lynn Morgan and Conrad Haigh,
Transport for London

An effective transport policy is key to the efficient operation of many public and private sector organizations. Increasingly, organizations are developing and implementing *travel plans* to address the traffic impacts of their activities – and are reaping the wide-ranging benefits that they can bring.

A 2004 British Chamber of Commerce (BCC) transport survey identified that the cost incurred as a result of problems with the UK's transport system equated to an average of £27,000 per BCC member business per year. The total cost to the UK economy of problems with the transport infrastructure was calculated at £15 billion.

The government's *Quality of Life Counts* report (update 2004) provisionally estimated total road traffic in 2003 to be 20 per cent higher than in 1990 and 7 per cent higher than in 1998. It has more than doubled since 1970.

If no action is taken, road traffic will continue to increase, bringing yet more problems and increased costs to UK business – as well as associated problems such as increased pollution. The development and implementation of workplace travel plans is one of the tools that can be used to help tackle the ever-increasing problem of congestion on our roads.

What is a travel plan?

A travel plan is a management tool involving the introduction of a package of measures aimed at reducing car use and promoting greener, cleaner travel choices within an organization. A travel plan may address some or all of the following:

■ staff travel to and from work;
■ staff travel in the course of work;
■ visitor travel to an organization's sites;
■ use of fleet vehicles;
■ deliveries and contractor movements.

A successful travel plan is based upon staff consultation and involves an ongoing process of monitoring and review. Measures implemented as part of the plan should address the full range of transport modes, ie walking, cycling, public transport use, car use, etc, in order to maximize travel choice. Research has shown that, to be effective, travel plans should include 'incentives' such as improved cycle parking as well as 'disincentives' such as a robust parking policy that could involve charging for parking or prioritization of spaces based upon a set of needs-based criteria.

Pharmaceutical giant GlaxoSmithKline (GSK) is an example of one company that has introduced an extremely effective travel plan. The company has had a presence in Brentford in west London for 60 years, and in October 2001 it relocated its corporate worldwide headquarters to the A4 in Brentford. The move meant that the organization would no longer be able to meet the demand for car parking from staff, with 3,000 staff working on-site and just over 1,000 parking spaces available. Thus, GSK introduced a travel plan to help address the potential shortfall in parking provision by making it easier for staff to travel to work by alternatives to the car.

GSK's transport challenges were met in a variety of ways through a mix of both standard and innovative techniques, including:

■ introduction of a car-share partner-matching scheme, including the offer of a guaranteed ride home to car sharers who were let down at the last minute by their car-sharing partner;
■ public transport season ticket loans;

- introduction of an on-site transport advice service offering one-to-one travel advice to staff;
- introduction of a robust car parking policy;
- introduction of a comprehensive cycling strategy;
- contribution to the redevelopment of the local railway station through planning agreements.

The most successful element of GSK's travel plan has been the Cycling Strategy, which included:

- installation of excellent high-quality showering, changing and locker facilities for staff;
- high-quality cycle parking facilities for over 300 cycles;
- introduction of a 'bike miles' scheme, which acts in a similar way to a supermarket loyalty card, whereby cyclists can accrue points whenever they cycle to work for purchase of cycle equipment.

The Cycling Strategy has won a number of awards, including the London Cycling Campaign 2002 Best Workplace Cycling Activity Award; the Cyclists' Touring Club 2003 National Award; the London Transport Award 2004 Most Innovative Scheme; the 2005 British Institute of Facilities Management Innovation Award; and a highly commended 2005 Liveable Cities Award in recognition of the organization's 'outstanding contribution to Traffic Reduction and Transport Management'.

Registered cyclists have increased from 50 to 350 since 2001 – an impressive sevenfold increase – and numbers continue to rise. GSK estimates that each cyclist costs the organization £400 per annum, which compares very favourably to the cost of renting car park spaces, estimated at over £2,000 per annum. Cycling also supports GSK's mission statement: 'Enabling people to do more, feel better and live longer.'

Samira Khan oversees the travel plan and says:

> The travel plan was implemented to meet a business need – we simply were not allowed to provide parking for all of our staff when we moved to this new site in 2001. However, the benefits that have been delivered by the plan have been very welcome and, in some cases, surprising. We have made significant cost savings on parking, and have a healthier workforce. There have been times, of course, when it has been challenging but we have worked with staff to achieve something that works for all of us.

Why should an organization develop a travel plan?

There are a number of reasons why an organization may develop a travel plan:

- *To secure planning permission:* These days, a good travel plan is generally an essential requirement of planning permission. So, if an organization has expansion plans or is relocating, it is highly likely that the local authority granting the permission will require a travel plan to be developed and implemented for the site.

■ *To help solve car parking problems:*
 – For organizations where car parking is at, or close to, capacity, with little opportunity to expand, a travel plan can reduce the demand for parking, thereby doing away with the need to find and pay for alternative parking.
 – An organization may consider the operating costs of its car parks to be too high, and it may want to reduce demand for parking in order to cut back on car park maintenance costs.
 – An organization may be losing car parking spaces because of further development, or may be moving to a new location where fewer spaces are available. A travel plan can help mitigate the impact of the reduction in parking availability, as in the case of GSK.
 – An organization may wish to reallocate spaces, with, for example, more spaces available to visitors and customers and fewer spaces for staff. A travel plan can help to manage this change effectively.
■ *To improve accessibility:* Traffic congestion both on-site and on local roads has economic costs associated with it in terms of fuel costs, time spent by staff in queuing traffic, extra costs of moving goods, etc. A travel plan therefore helps an organization operate more efficiently.
■ *To improve an organization's environmental image:* With increasing concern for environmental issues, a travel plan can demonstrate an organization's commitment to reducing the travel impact of its activities, making it a 'good neighbour' and an 'employer of choice'. A travel plan can link well to environmental accreditation schemes such as ISO 14001 and the Eco-Management and Audit Scheme (EMAS), or to an organization's corporate social responsibility agenda.

To address its travel issues, the BBC has developed travel plans for a number of sites across the UK to reduce unnecessary travel where possible. The key drivers behind travel planning at the BBC have been:

■ to support the BBC's environmental policy;
■ to counteract the reduction in parking spaces as a result of new development, for example the travel plan developed for its White City development in London;
■ to meet the requirement to produce travel plans as part of Section 106 planning agreements for new developments;
■ to reduce expenditure on travel, especially on taxis; and
■ to show care for employees.

Shuttle buses have been introduced as part of the BBC's travel plan policy and operate between Television Centre (W1) and Broadcasting House (W12). It is estimated that introduction of the shuttle has saved 2,000 journeys per week, and the service currently carries approximately 300 passengers per day, many of whom would previously have made their journeys by car or taxi. The BBC has also provided cycle racks, shower facilities and drying facilities, and a rigorous parking allocation policy has been introduced. The percentage of staff travelling by car in inner London was reduced from 28 per cent in 1999 to 10–11 per cent in 2005.

Andrew Fullerton, Head of Environmental Planning at the BBC, said:

> As well as their journeys to work, a high proportion of our staff and contributors make trips either between business premises or to other locations during their working day. Fewer private car park spaces are available as a result of our own site developments and those of third parties. This has reduced our overhead costs but made it all the more important that we work with other stakeholders, including public transport providers, and exploit new technology to provide our staff with a range of options which either reduce their need to travel or improve the convenience of alternative modes. Over the past five years this has resulted in lower costs, less environmental impact and more choice for staff.

What benefits can a travel plan bring?

A travel plan can bring a number of benefits to an organization and, therefore, even if a company is not formally required to develop a travel plan as a requirement of planning, serious consideration should be given to 'voluntary' travel plan development.

An *organization* can benefit from increased productivity generated by a healthier, more motivated workforce, reduced congestion, reduced demand for parking and improved access for staff, visitors and deliveries. Importantly, a travel plan can also reduce an organization's overhead costs, including savings on:

- the maintenance costs of car parking;
- office space requirements, for example as a result of a policy to encourage increased homeworking;
- business travel costs as a result of, for example, new working practices that reduce the need to travel, such as introduction of videoconferencing facilities;
- staff costs, including reduced sick leave (and reduced agency costs to cover staff off sick) as a result of a healthier, more motivated workforce;
- taxis and couriers; and
- fleet and associated on-costs such as insurance.

A travel plan can also help to widen the potential labour pool by increasing travel choice and can create a more attractive recruitment package, which can aid both recruitment and retention. Indeed, in a 2003 report by the Social Exclusion Unit entitled *Making Connections*, 38 per cent of jobseekers said that transport (lack of personal transport or public transport) is a key barrier to getting a job, with 13 per cent of people saying they had not applied for a particular job in the preceding 12 months because of transport problems. Clearly, therefore, a travel plan can form an important part of any organization's business plan, and can also help it improve its competitive edge.

Staff can benefit from improved health, cost and time savings and reduced stress.

The *local community* can benefit from reduced congestion, reduced journey times, improved public transport services, safer roads and reduced parking in residential areas.

The *environment* generally can benefit from improved air quality, less noise and less pollution.

BAA Heathrow introduced workplace travel planning in 2000 to ease congestion and car parking constraints and to help reduce emissions. Not only have the plans proved successful in meeting business needs but they have also enabled BAA Heathrow to make significant savings:

■ £8 million was saved in 2002/03 by deferring the building of a multi-deck car park and by reducing demand for staff car parking spaces by 500 daily at Heathrow.
■ Videoconferencing was introduced across the BAA Group, and in less than one year the initial investment cost of £150,000 was recouped.
■ Alternative work styles, eg hot-desking, have allowed the release of accommodation, with a cost saving of *circa* £400,000 per annum.
■ The airport car share initiative has been a resounding success. Since the scheme was introduced in April 2001 across the seven BAA UK airports:
    – 4,816,561 litres of fuel has been saved, equating to £4,938 per person;
    – 7,835 members of staff have registered on the scheme, from 436 different companies;
    – There has been a 45,840,400-kilometre reduction in the distance driven by staff;
    – There has been a 9,538,595-kilogram reduction in the amount of CO_2 produced.

(These figures are based on two people sharing three days a week and making a round trip of 69 kilometres. Figures accurate as at April 2005.)

Promoting travel plans in London

In London, Ken Livingstone, Mayor of London, has actively supported the development and implementation of travel plans. In a news release prior to a Central London Partnership event for London businesses ('Business on the move: travel planning is the smarter choice for London businesses'), the Mayor said:

London is the fastest growing major city in Europe. That is a testament to our dynamism and success. To sustain London's growth and prosperity we have to expand the city's transport system and are working to ensure that those assets we already have are used with the maximum efficiency. Business travel plans can make a big difference to ensuring we get the most out of our transport system and that businesses start the day efficiently by helping employees plan the most reliable and healthy journey to work.

Transport for London, with its remit of implementing the Mayor of London's transport strategy and managing transport services across the capital, is working in partnership with London boroughs actively to promote travel plans amongst businesses, universities and colleges, NHS trusts and other organizations. Transport for London's travel plan support to organizations includes:

■ the appointment of 11 sub-regional travel plan coordinators across London to help organizations develop and implement effective travel plans;
■ financial assistance in implementing travel plan measures;
■ development of a comprehensive travel plan monitoring tool (iTRACE) to enable the take-up and effectiveness of travel plans in London to be monitored;
■ production of a range of good-practice guidance for travel plan development and practical implementation;
■ contributions to funding car share schemes and some car clubs. All boroughs are covered by an area-wide car share scheme, and car clubs cover a number of boroughs throughout London.

The potential contribution that workplace travel plans could make towards reducing congestion is significant. A Department for Transport study published in December 2004, entitled *Making Smarter Choices Work*, concluded that an intensive 'smarter choices' programme could reduce urban peak-hour traffic by 21 per cent. 'Smarter choices' include:

■ school and workplace travel plans;
■ individualized marketing (or personalized travel planning);
■ improved public transport information and marketing;
■ car sharing;
■ car clubs; and
■ the encouragement of teleworking and teleconferencing.

The research found that measures targeting the journey to work (workplace travel plans, car sharing and teleworking) could deliver about half of this reduction.

Clearly, therefore, workplace travel plans in both the public and the private sector have a key role to play in delivering a more sustainable transport network, not just in London but throughout the UK – whilst at the same time bringing significant benefits to organizations themselves.

Effective fleet management: reducing costs, helping the environment

Conrad Haigh, Transport for London

Transport and the environment

Carbon dioxide (CO_2) is the most important greenhouse gas, accounting for around 86 per cent of the UK's total emissions in 2003. It is a major cause of global warming, one of the greatest environmental challenges facing the world today. Rising global temperatures will bring changes in weather patterns, rising sea levels and increased frequency and intensity of extreme weather events. The effects will be felt in the UK, and internationally there may be severe problems for people in regions that are particularly vulnerable to change.

In 2003, industry and the transport sector each accounted for just over 28 per cent of CO_2 emissions, whilst domestic users accounted for a further 27 per cent.

Between 1970 and 2003, total CO_2 emissions fell by 19 per cent. Much of this decline has come from a reduction in emissions attributable to industry (which have declined by almost half since 1970) and emissions caused by domestic users (which have declined by 24 per cent since 1970). However, CO_2 emissions attributable to transport have increased by 89 per cent since 1970, as illustrated in Figure 3.3.1.

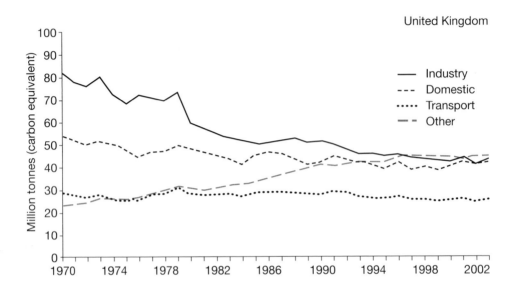

Source: netcen

Figure 3.3.1 Carbon dioxide emissions by end user, 1970–2003

Although improvements in vehicle technology have led to dramatic reductions in the exhaust emissions that cause poor air quality, there has been less progress on reducing CO_2 emissions. The *average* fuel consumption of new cars sold today is similar to the average of those sold in the mid-1980s, despite significant improvements in the fuel efficiency achieved by comparable engines (see Figure 3.3.2). This is because there has been an increase in average vehicle size and weight over the same period as a result of a number of factors, including improved crash protection, the widespread addition of features such as power-assisted steering and air-conditioning, and consumers choosing larger and more powerful models.

Transport and health

Road transport is also one of the major sources of emissions that are harmful to human health, including oxides of nitrogen (NO_x) and fine particles, both of which can have an adverse impact on people suffering from respiratory illnesses such as asthma. Indeed, fine particles have been associated with increased hospital admissions and in bringing forward the deaths of those with respiratory illnesses.

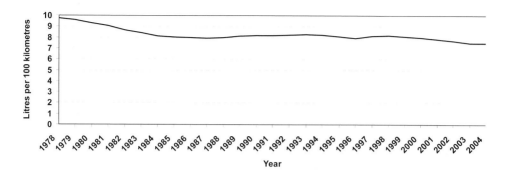

Note: Registration-weighted; petrol two-wheel-drive vehicles only

Source: Cleaner Fuels and Vehicles Division, DfT

Figure 3.3.2   New car fuel consumption, 1978–2004

In London, during 2005 it was estimated that road transport accounted for 47 per cent of fine particle and 47 per cent of NO_X emissions. These emissions tend to be more of an issue in London because of the high traffic volumes and low traffic speeds. Moreover, poor dispersion conditions because of the built-up nature of the city further increase the impact and exposure levels.

Government action to reduce harmful emissions

Although the total quantity of CO_2 has been declining in the UK, the predicted increase in car use and greater distances travelled could outweigh the benefits gained from technological advances unless real action is taken to address this. The government is convinced that action to reduce harmful emissions and reduce the adverse environmental effects of transport must continue.

The government's approach to tackling air pollution is set out in the Air Quality Strategy for England, Scotland, Wales and Northern Ireland. The strategy identifies the action required at a national and international level, and the contribution that industry, transport and local government can make to ensure objectives are met. In response to this, proposals for the introduction of a low emission zone (LEZ) for Greater London are being drawn up. The aim is to discourage older, more polluting vehicles from driving within London in order to reduce road transport emissions and improve air quality. The earliest possible implementation date of an LEZ in London is early 2008.

'Greening' vehicle fleets

Increasingly, organizations are looking at how they can 'green' their vehicle fleets, with either the environmental impact of their fleet providing the stimulus for improvements or commercial factors providing the motivation for fleet improvements; if a fleet is not effectively managed, excess costs of up to 35 per cent can be incurred.

Even if fleet managers aim to improve fleet performance on purely commercial or cost-efficiency grounds, this will almost always involve better fuel economy and lower emissions, so the environmental and health gains will come as a bonus anyway. For many fleets the financial gains to be made will outweigh any of the implementation costs, typically within 24–36 months, and the environmental benefits will already have started to make an impact well within this time-frame.

Green fleet management and rationalization of deliveries can also bring other benefits, including reduced congestion, fewer accidents and less noise and severance of communities.

Increasingly, the 'greening' of a vehicle fleet is being integrated into the development and implementation of a workplace travel plan as part of a much wider organizational transport policy, as outlined in the final paragraph of this chapter.

What is green fleet management?

Green fleet management means much more than undertaking an occasional review of fuel consumption. A green fleet programme aims to increase fuel efficiency and reduce vehicle emissions and should include measures to:

■ *Reduce fuel consumption.* With typical fuel costs accounting for around 25–30 per cent of the total operating costs of a fleet, managing fuel use makes sound commercial sense. However, fuel costs are not fixed overheads and will vary according to factors such as vehicle type, driving style and mileage. An effective fuel management process can save around 10 per cent of fuel costs.

■ *Reduce mileage.* The 'greenest' mile of all is the one that is not driven, and organizations should manage the routeing and scheduling of their trips to minimize mileage. Reducing mileage has the added impact of reducing emissions, fuel consumption, the risk of accidents, and the contribution the organization is making towards congestion.

■ *Provide training in fuel-efficient driving techniques.* Driving style has a huge influence on fuel consumption, with aggressive driving behaviour adding up to 45 per cent to fuel bills. It will also increase wear and tear on a vehicle and, furthermore, the driver who wastes fuel is also likely to be the driver who has more accidents. Formal driver training can bring significant benefits but should include a regular refresher course so that improvements are sustained. A fuel economy bonus scheme can also be a powerful motivator for drivers to try to conserve fuel.

■ *Use cleaner fuels and gradually replace the fleet with low-emissions vehicles.* A range of cleaner vehicle technologies and alternative fuels is now available, giving fleet managers a number of options for improving the environmental performance of their vehicles. However, there is no one single vehicle or fuel that can be applied to all fleets. Choices need to take account of a number of factors, in particular the individual operational requirements of the fleet and local environmental factors, such as whether there are air quality problems in the areas in which vehicles operate.

The future introduction of LEZs in some city centres, or the introduction of congestion charging, is also an important commercial factor to consider when choosing a fleet vehicle. If a business needs vehicular access to premises inside an LEZ, for example, it will need to consider how it will be able to achieve this once the schemes are introduced. Using only vehicles that conform to the latest European standards may be one way; using alternatively fuelled vehicles could be another.

Whitbread Group plc introduced a green fleet strategy in 1999 as part of its overall environmental strategy. The strategy included monitoring fuel use and mileage, identifying poorly performing vehicles and drivers, using incentives and disincentives to influence vehicle choice, and investing in alternatives for business travel such as videoconferencing and car sharing. In 2002, Whitbread estimated that it was saving well in excess of £200,000 per annum, with the fleet producing 1,600 tonnes of CO_2 less than it would have done had the vehicle fleet been the same size as in 1999.

In the UK, local authorities can lead by example, and many are adopting a clean fleet strategy with a supporting travel plan as part of a package of measures adopted in their air quality strategy. Islington Council operates a fleet of around 400 vehicles, including 18 LPG vehicles, 3 electric vehicles and 16 electric scooters. Around 10 per cent of the fleet runs on alternative fuels, and the council has introduced a vehicle replacement programme planned until 2009 to incorporate the latest 'green' technology and to ensure that a low fleet average age is maintained.

The council has also developed a system of evaluating the environmental performance as well as the financial implication of running each of its vehicles. As different fuels and vehicle technologies have varying prices and are eligible for discounts on vehicle excise duty, the system enables the council to evaluate the best replacement option.

Southwark Council has also been recognized for its green fleet. The council has around 310 company cars and 300 other fleet vehicles, ranging from small car-derived vans to refuse collection vehicles. The council has demonstrated that any comprehensive green fleet management strategy must be embedded in a council's corporate culture with the full acknowledgement and support of staff throughout the organization.

Not only has the council had the benefit of showing its residents that it is a responsible authority but it has realized a potential saving of over £100,000 in congestion charges with the utilization of LPG alone. Southwark's green fleet strategy has a number of elements, including:

■ an alternative fuel policy that ensures that the existing petrol fleet is replaced over time with similar vehicles converted to LPG;
■ 65 vehicles running on a 20 per cent biodiesel blend;
■ an awareness-raising programme to ensure the council gains the support of its workforce;

- a driver training programme focused on fuel-efficient driving techniques;
- a vehicle procurement policy that ensures that an exact fuel type or vehicle is specified for each operational need. This includes the adoption of the latest European standards for each vehicle type and the use of LPG and biodiesel fuels where applicable.

Assistance available to 'green' vehicle fleets

TransportEnergy, a division of the government-funded Energy Saving Trust, provides information that aims to create more sustainable transport solutions through independent advice on green fleet management (visit www.transportenergy.co.uk for further information).

In addition, the Carbon Trust, a government-funding organization, works with businesses and the public sector to help them reduce their carbon emissions. A number of councils throughout the UK, including Southwark, Lewisham and Croydon, are already benefiting from the initiative.

Furthermore, as part of its programme of encouraging further development and implementation of travel plans, Transport for London is encouraging organizations to consider measures to 'green' their fleet. As part of this, the Travel Demand Management Team will be launching a practical guide on choosing the correct vehicle and fuel type for an organization's operations. The guide has been produced in conjunction with Momenta, a division of AEA Technology.

Health and safety: legal overview

James Taylor, Simmons & Simmons

Health and safety is an area where there is a long-established legislative regime – the Health and Safety at Work Act 1974 and the numerous regulations and approved codes of practice. Some, but not all, of the legislation is derived from European legislation. In 2004, HM Treasury set a new health and safety public service agreement (PSA), which includes targets for the Health and Safety Executive (HSE). The Health and Safety Commission (HSC) Business Plan for 2005–08 introduces two main strategic delivery programmes (SDPs) as the main agent for delivering the HSC strategy and the PSA targets, which are 'Fit for work, fit for life, fit for tomorrow' (Fit 3) and 'Major hazards'. These two SDPs are supported by four strategic enabling programmes (Business involvement, Worker involvement, Local authority/HSE partnership, and Enforcement).

The Fit 3 SDP aims to deliver a 3 per cent reduction in the incidence of work-related fatal and major injuries (concentrating on slips and trips, falls, construction and workplace transport); a 6 per cent reduction in the incidence rate of cases of work-related ill health (concentrating on musculoskeletal disorders, stress, noise and vibration, skin diseases, asthma and health support); and a 9 per cent reduction in the incidence rate of days lost due to work-related injuries and ill health (concentrating on the public sector and raising the profile of sickness absence management). The Major hazards SDP focuses on the HSE's work regulating and ensuring safe management of those industries where failure to manage risks to health and safety could have catastrophic effects. Stakeholder engagement and communication are a major part of the delivery of improved health.

In 2005 it was noticeable that the courts handed out some very high fines in respect of health and safety offences, and this shows the increasing willingness of the courts to hear the HSE's repeated calls for higher fines to act as a greater deterrent. The government is currently consulting on legislation creating a new offence of corporate manslaughter in which it aims to remove the current legal difficulties in identifying the controlling mind of an organization. The trade unions are actively lobbying on this Bill, and they are looking for imprisonment of directors as a potential penalty, something that the original Bill did not provide for.

Occupational health and safety

Errol Taylor, The Royal Society for the Prevention of Accidents (RoSPA)

The business case

> Society as a whole pays when things go wrong. We estimate that the total cost to society of health and safety failures could be as high as £18 billion every year. We can and should do something about this.
>
> (John Prescott, UK Deputy Prime Minister, 2000)

At a macroeconomic level there is substantial evidence that poor health and safety practices represent a significant cost to the economy and that improving occupational health and safety has a positive impact on economic performance. However, the costs to employers are hidden by the fact that the National Health Service (NHS) provides free treatment at the point of delivery. Costs only become visible in the form of insatiable demands for NHS funding through the taxpayer.

Much progress has been made in this field, but the UK Department for Work and Pensions, in its report on employee liability insurance, noted that 'Our safety performance in the UK is good – that is one reason why the costs of employers' liability are still much lower than our international competitors'. But there is more to be done, particularly on occupational health.'

Accidents and injuries grab the headlines, and inevitably companies focus on prevention in the form of various high-profile safety initiatives. Performance can be benchmarked through schemes like the CHASPI index, and the very highest standards can be celebrated by winning awards such as RoSPA's Sir George Earl Trophy. The United Kingdom's Health and Safety Executive (HSE) is now keen to shift the focus to health. While health is less spectacular, the social and economic damage caused by work-related ill health is in many ways more significant than that caused by accidents. Stress, bad backs, repetitive stress injury (RSI) and other largely work-related conditions are estimated to affect some 2 million workers in the United Kingdom.

Securing Health Together, a report by the HSE launched in 2000, states:

> Despite good progress in reducing the number of accidents at work, Great Britain still needs to strive to achieve similar success in tackling the current high levels of work-related ill health. We need a long-term occupational health strategy for several reasons: to stop people being made ill by work; to help people who are ill go back to work; and to improve work opportunities for those not able to work because of ill health or disability.

Defined within the Occupational Health and Safety Assessment series of standards as 'the conditions and factors that affect the well-being of employees, temporary workers, contractor personnel, visitors and any other person in the workplace', occupational health and safety affects every workplace, employee and employer.

Manley considers the United Kingdom's NHS and provides the following example of the significant benefits of conducting sound occupational health practices:

> In the NHS bad backs are common causes of absenteeism and nurses scarce and difficult to replace – with temporary nurses a significant drain on resources. One NHS trust, Wigan and Leigh, with 5000 staff, decided to address the problem. In 1993 they commissioned a report into sickness among staff and found 44,000 hrs/yr were lost at an estimated cost £3.9 million. Losses due to industrial injuries were 11,635 hrs/yr, with nurses most commonly affected, and heavy lifting a key reason. They then developed a comprehensive package to address the problem, involving risk assessment, training risk assessors, purchasing equipment, and educating staff. The non-staff costs were £80,000 in the first year, £50,000 in the second. The results were that time lost due to lifting injuries fell from 6720 hours to 1082 in the first year, with further reductions in subsequent years until only 192 hours were lost. The cost of this lost time fell from £800,000 to £24,000.

> (M Manley, 2002, *Health and Safety Indicators for Institutional Investors*,
> HSE, London)

Statistics published in the *Occupational Health Statistics Bulletin* 2002/03 show that an estimated 33 million working days were lost from the UK economy. The two main causes were, first, stress, depression and anxiety and, second, musculoskeletal disorders, resulting in 13.4 million and 12.3 million days lost respectively (see Figure 3.5.1).

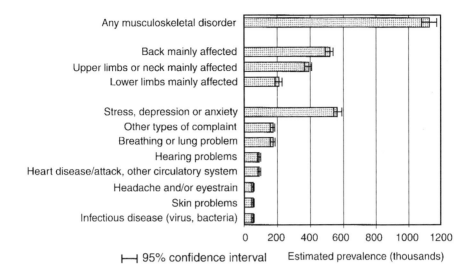

Source: National Statistics, *Occupational Health Statistics Bulletin*, 2002/03

Figure 3.5.1   Causes of lost working days in the United Kingdom

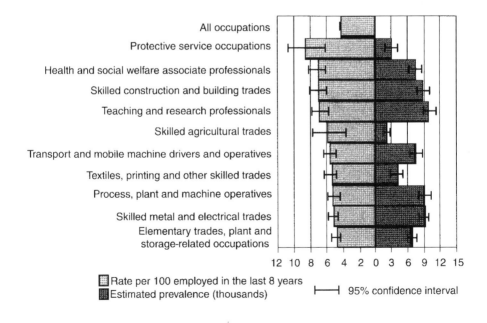

Source: National Statistics, *Occupational Health Statistics Bulletin*, 2002/03

Figure 3.5.2   Relationship between illness levels and occupation

Further review of the statistics shows the relationship between illness levels and occupations. Police officers and nurses have the highest levels, followed by builders, teachers and agricultural workers (see Figure 3.5.2).

Occupations appear to have very distinct risk profiles that cause specific types of illnesses. The fight against crime exposes police officers to violent individuals, resulting in injuries in the line of duty. Lifting heavy and awkward patients means that back pain is commonplace among nurses. Unruly pupils, constant change and high workload mean that teachers suffer from stress.

Occupational health and safety can no longer be viewed as the exclusive domain of a small team of 'OHS' experts. All employees and organizations are affected, and risk profiles can have a significant impact on the bottom line. A poor safety record means that today's insurance premiums will be high. Tomorrow, the business may no longer be viable, and a brand that has taken many years to create might be destroyed overnight by hostile publicity. All other factors being equal, who would choose to travel with an airline known to have a poor safety record or buy a new car with low Euro NCAP crash test ratings?

Legislators and regulators

The World Health Organization (WHO) recognizes occupational health as one of its fundamental priorities, and has set out a global strategy with eight major priority areas:

■ strengthening of international and national policies for health at work;
■ promotion of a healthy work environment, healthy work practices and health at work;
■ strengthening of occupational health services;
■ establishment of appropriate support services for occupational health;
■ development of occupational health standards based on scientific risk assessment;
■ development of human resources;
■ establishment of registration and data systems and information support;
■ strengthening of research.

Occupational health is a fundamental part of the European Union's strategy on safety and health at work. This is made apparent in communications from the European Commission. A Community strategy on health and safety at work in the period 2002–06 advocates that we adopt a global approach to well-being at work, taking account of changes in the world of work and the emergence of new risks, especially of a psychosocial nature. With its work on bullying and violence at the workplace, and consultation with social partners on the issue of stress-related conditions, the Commission is establishing stress as a key issue in the management of occupational health and safety.

Following a series of high-profile accidents on Britain's rail network, there is growing public concern at the lack of success of UK criminal law in convicting companies of manslaughter where a death has occurred as a result of gross negligence by the organization as a whole. The debate on accountability rages, with the government and many business leaders preferring to hold organizations to account through the Corporate Manslaughter Bill, while critics continue to argue the case for a sharper focus on individual directors.

The investors' perspective

Historically, most pension funds have had little focus on health, safety and environmental issues. However, recent pension fund regulation on the topic of disclosure has meant that both the pension fund and the investment management communities are more interested in socially responsible investments.

Mainstream pension funds now expect the boards of companies in which they invest to work to the spirit of the Turnbull guidelines – that is, they expect the boards to have considered and be actively managing risks associated with these issues. (The Turnbull Report, *Internal Control: Guidance for directors on the Combined Code*, was issued by the Institute of Chartered Accountants in England and Wales (ICAEW) in 1999.) Occasionally, fund managers may raise social and environmental issues with companies, checking that the board is properly managing such issues.

A smaller but growing number of funds take social and environmental issues into account when they are selecting companies for their investment portfolios. Their concern can be driven from one of two perspectives: ethical funds require exemplary management of social and environmental issues as a prerequisite, while other investors see them as indicators of well-managed businesses. This is of particular interest where health and safety data can be linked to financial performance.

From a negative perspective, investors consider that poor health and safety risk management suggests a generally weak approach to risk management and therefore an increased financial risk of unexpected liabilities. It can also be seen as an indicator of employee morale and the respect shown by the company to staff, potentially linking to the concept of measuring human capital and the state of corporate culture.

A clear message from investors is that they do not see themselves as 'police' in this area. A growing number of investors are concerned that they are being pressurized by government to 'enforce' health and safety within companies.

The skills gap

The WHO paper *The Way to Health at Work* (1994) acknowledges that occupational health means far more than providing conventional primary health care to workers (and at the workplace). Occupational health is a preventive activity aiming at identification, assessment and control of hazardous factors at the workplace, and the generation of competent and effective actions to ensure a healthy work environment and healthy workers. Such activity cannot be carried out with primary health care competence alone; specialized occupational health competence and knowledge of the real needs of working life are necessary (eg knowledge on industrial and other chemicals, physical factors at work, ergonomics, safety, work psychology and occupational medicine).

It is apparent that the scope of occupational health embraces a wide variety of issues, skills and competencies, much more so than what are traditionally labelled 'safety issues'. The health and safety professional needs to be fully aware of these issues; they cannot be ignored, as statistics show that ill health is now a much larger problem to tackle than in the past. The majority of health and safety professionals have experience of having worked in industries with high-profile safety risks, such as nuclear, construction and petrochemicals, not necessarily the industries carrying the highest health risks (transport, food and waste). With the rise of the service sector, bringing issues such as the increase of peripatetic working and emergence of issues such as occupational road risk, stress and violence, awareness and knowledge need to be increased. Professional bodies and stakeholders are recognizing this and responding.

The Confederation of British Industry advocated in December 2001 that business management of occupational health and rehabilitation should be improved, remarking that 30 per cent of employers do not give occupational health provision. Unfortunately, a subsequent report on preventive services, prepared by Laurent Vogel and published in the *TUTB Newsletter* of June 2003, paints a rather damning picture. Although the report embodies a trade union slant, it suggests that the number of UK workers with access to preventive services has fallen 'dramatically'. Specialized health and safety staffs exist in about half the firms with organized prevention activities, and it claims that companies 'do not have the development of preventative services as a priority'.

Management attitudes

Given that business schools can be considered as the source of the next generation of business leaders, it is perhaps surprising that so little time is devoted to the topic of health and safety. Study of the coverage of occupational health and safety on full-time MBA courses in business schools in Great Britain was commissioned by the HSE, which found that 'the explicit occupational health and safety content of the eight MBAs was either non-existent or very limited' and that 'MBA staff tended to think that occupational health and safety was vitally important in major hazard industries but a bureaucratic, legalistic imposition for most other organisations'. Even where they recognized that occupational health and safety was an important corporate goal, business educators had not fully made the link between safety management and the management skills taught on MBA programmes. They questioned the academic rigour of the subject, and did not perceive occupational health and safety as a topic worthy of inclusion in a postgraduate course.

Fortunately, employers are generally beginning to take a more enlightened attitude towards the subject. For example, the Engineering Employers' Federation (EEF) recognizes that occupational health is a serious issue for UK manufacturing and engineering companies; it appointed a chief medical adviser in 2002 and has in place an occupational health strategy: 'The EEF's Occupational Health Strategy carries the broad aim of improving the health of companies and their employees, presenting and championing the business case for occupational health. Our campaigning in this area will engage the EEF more in policy development and profile on many issues including workplace stress, absence management, rehabilitation, management development.'

Tools, techniques and standards

Research by Manley (2002), mentioned earlier, suggests that companies should report against the following set of indicators to demonstrate best-practice levels of health and safety management. These indicators have been chosen because they satisfy the data needs of investors while offering comparability across various economic sectors. They provide a broad overview of health and safety performance at a company level, and should allow investors to work out whether the issues are being managed appropriately:

1. appointment of a director with the responsibility of being the health and safety champion;
2. the levels at which health and safety management systems are reported;
3. number of fatalities;
4. lost-time injury rate;
5. absenteeism rate;
6. cost of health and safety losses.

A standard methodology needs to be agreed to calculate and report indicators 4, 5 and 6, with significant input from qualified accountants on indicator 6.

Organizations are generally able to identify and calculate the direct costs associated with injury and illness, but they find it far more difficult to relate specific incidents to indirect costs borne by separate departments (see Figure 3.5.3). These include lost production caused by an accident, lost revenue where a client cancels a delayed order, and damage to tangible assets, including product and plant. Indirect costs can be between 6 and 53 times as large as the direct costs. A company that has lost £20,000 in one year because of injury and illness costs will typically incur additional losses of £120,000–£1,060,000. The scale of the costs will depend on the type of industry in which the organization operates.

Meanwhile, the environmental standard ISO 14001 and the occupational health and safety system OHSAS 18001 have introduced the concept of a risk-based approach to management systems standards. The standards are designed to enable organizations to identify, evaluate and manage the risks they face, through reduction and elimination of those risks.

As a result of adopting these process- and risk-based approaches, organizations improve their focus on the requirements and expectations of their stakeholders, including customers, regulators and employees. They are also in a better position to manage the way in which they interact with their physical environment as well as looking after the health and safety of people at work. Thanks to the use of performance

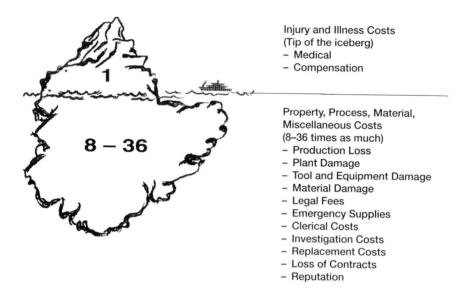

Injury and Illness Costs
(Tip of the iceberg)
– Medical
– Compensation

Property, Process, Material,
Miscellaneous Costs
(8–36 times as much)
– Production Loss
– Plant Damage
– Tool and Equipment Damage
– Material Damage
– Legal Fees
– Emergency Supplies
– Clerical Costs
– Investigation Costs
– Replacement Costs
– Loss of Contracts
– Reputation

Figure 3.5.3   The cost of loss iceberg

measures, organizations can measure progress against objectives, a process that in turn can be used to help drive continual improvement, competitiveness and therefore success in an increasingly demanding environment (see Figure 3.5.4).

The use by organizations of OHSAS 18001, the occupational health and safety management system specification, demonstrates that they have identified hazards and performed a risk assessment relating to personnel and facilities in the workplace, as well as having put in place programmes to manage these risks. Organizations working in this way address another key group of stakeholders – the people within the organization – helping to establish a culture of risk management. The use of a quantitative methodology allows performance benchmarking year on year or site against site and provides the data to allow top management to drive the continuous improvement cycle.

RoSPA's pioneering work to raise the profile of occupational road risk has highlighted the fact that today's employees face far bigger risks on the road than in the workplace, driving as part of their job. Commercial organizations use company vehicles as large mobile advertisements to promote themselves and their key messages. When such vehicles are involved in a road traffic accident, the cost of adverse publicity is incalculable and probably far higher than the obvious costs of damage and downtime. Effective management of occupational road risk isn't just a case of training drivers: it requires a comprehensive approach starting with corporate objectives and policies, a review of management culture and accident data, eliminating unnecessary travel and an assessment of individual drivers' risk profiles. Resources can then be allocated to reduce the risk profile both to employees and to the organization.

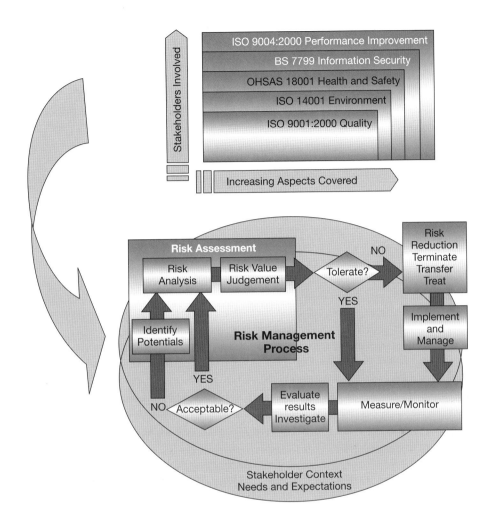

Figure 3.5.4 The drive for continual improvement

Conclusion

Harming employees is socially unacceptable and increasingly expensive. Legislation has meant that safety in the workplace has received a considerable amount of attention and accident rates are being driven down. The Corporate Manslaughter Bill will reinforce the need to take safety seriously at board level. Similarly, tough safety requirements are being built into products to ensure that they won't harm the user. Building on this success, the focus of policy makers now is switching to risk management in the context of occupational health and safety. Long-term chronic injuries caused by repeated exposure to apparently minor irritants, including dust, noise and stress, are now coming under the microscope. Insurers, investors, Turnbull and the Combined Code require companies to have clear systems for managing risks, reporting to stakeholders and shouldering responsibility.

Case 1: the food industry

Hardly a month goes by without another 'food scare' in the media. Is beef safe to eat? Will prawns give you cancer? Are miscarriages caused by coffee?

A food safety scare can start as an unexpected, isolated incident that can rapidly escalate as a result of the complex interrelationships between different parts of the vast food industry, which employs a quarter of the world's population. Food supply chains increasingly transcend national boundaries. Thanks to air travel and refrigeration, fresh meat, fruit and vegetables are shipped thousands of kilometres from producer to consumer.

Consumer expectations are becoming ever more demanding. Not only should the food industry provide safe and wholesome food without nasty surprises, but it is coming under increasing ethical and emotional pressure for food that meets specific consumer values and preferences, whether it be food that is organic, health-enhancing, not genetically modified, low-carbohydrate, low-salt or whatever else meets current concerns. So-called junk foods, with their relatively high levels of fat and sugar, are being blamed for making children obese.

The United Kingdom is one of very few countries that have a statutory 'due diligence' defence requirement within their legislative framework. The Food Safety Act 1990 puts emphasis on 'due diligence', requiring all companies in the food chain to take reasonable precautions and exercise due diligence.

In response to UK food safety legislation, organizations such as the British Retail Consortium (BRC) have played a central role in developing standards on food safety within their supply chains to help retailers assure themselves that the food they sell is safe. Examples of this are the BRC technical standard for food and the BRC/Institute of Packaging standard for packaging. Fundamental to BRC standards are the premises that top management is responsible for food safety and that all food safety programmes should be built on a foundation of prerequisite programmes (PRPs) or good manufacturing practice (GMP) and the use of risk management approaches to managing food production. These standards are attempts to reduce the proliferation of standards applied by the different food retailers and are designed to allow an assessment, by a competent third party, of the supplier's premises, operational systems and procedures.

In May 2000 the Food Business Forum (CIES), an international trade association, established the Global Food Safety Initiative (GFSI), whose aims include enhancing food safety, ensuring consumer protection and strengthening consumer confidence. The GFSI task force's first priority has been to develop benchmark requirements for food safety schemes used in the retailer supply chains. These requirements are set out in the GFSI guidance document and establish key principles against which food safety schemes will be measured.

The GFSI task force brings together over 50 food retailers, which represent 65 per cent of the world's food retail revenue and include household names from the food retail and manufacturing and processing sector. Recently, the first tranche of food safety schemes have been determined as complying with the GFSI benchmark standard for food safety requirements. Key elements of the benchmark standard are a food safety management system, good practices, and hazard analysis and critical control points (HACCP). The schemes that comply are the BRC Technical Standard, the Dutch HACCP code, the EFSIS standard, the International Standard for Auditing Food Suppliers (International Food Standard) and the SQF 2000 code.

In 2001 the International Organization for Standardization (ISO) started work to develop a standard on food safety, ISO 22000: Food safety management systems. This standard is compatible with ISO 9001:2000 and specifies requirements for a food safety management system in the food chain. The key requirements are on communication within the food chain, system management, process controls, HACCP principles and good practice (or prerequisite programmes). ISO 22000 is based on codex, national standards and retailer food safety schemes. The harmonization of food safety schemes is set to continue.

Case 2: noise

Noise is an inevitable by-product from operating almost any piece of machinery. It can be continuous or percussive. Percussive sounds are usually unexpected, significantly louder than background noise, particularly noticeable and very difficult to absorb.

Percussive noise from equipment such as hydraulic jackhammers has an immediate effect on the hearing of the machinery operators. They suffer from temporary hearing loss and often suffer from a ringing sensation (tinnitus) for hours after exposure to the noise. Since the effects are so obvious, most operators are keen to wear earplugs or ear defenders to protect themselves. Usually people eventually recover most of their hearing. Explosions cause the most extreme form of this type of noise; the shock waves cause such brief but very high levels of noise that they can rupture the eardrums of unprotected listeners.

Continuous noise is more insidious and can cause long-term damage to hearing. The ear has the ability to adjust to the ambient level of any noise. This allows people to enter a noisy environment such as an engine room or discotheque, filter out most of the background noise and still be able to hear conversations. Unfortunately, repeated exposure leads to a gradual loss of hearing sensitivity, potentially culminating in complete deafness.

In the United States the National Institute of Occupational Safety and Health (NIOSH) claims that 30 million workers are exposed to hazardous levels of noise on the job and that noise-induced hearing loss is one of the most common occupational diseases. In the United Kingdom a recent survey estimated that over 500,000 people suffer from hearing difficulties as a result of exposure to noise at work. Industries with particularly high levels of noise include agriculture, mining, construction, manufacturing, utilities, transport and the military.

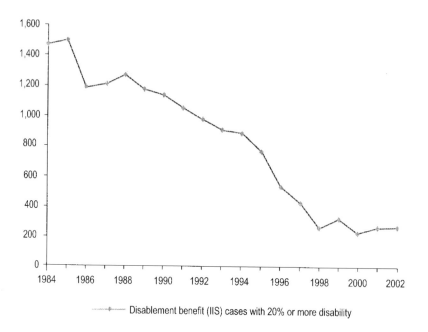

Source: www.hse.gov.uk/statistics/causdis/noise.htm

Figure 3.5.5   Cases of occupational deafness in the United Kingdom

Hearing loss is a significant handicap, as it reduces the ability to communicate with people or enjoy sounds such as music or birdsong. The costs in terms of disability settlements and medical treatment can be very high.

The good news is that hearing loss from these sources is 100 per cent preventable, and noise barriers can be relatively cheap. They range from earplugs and defenders for individual users to absorbent materials and acoustic barriers. A combination of legal enforcement and enlightened management has resulted in a sixfold decrease in cases of impaired hearing as a result of exposure to occupational noise (see Figure 3.5.5).

The business case for hearing conservation can be very attractive: between 1987 and 1997 the US military saved over $350 million as a result of a comprehensive conservation programme.

Case 3: stress

In today's 24/7 culture, with mobile telecommunications wherever you are in the world, workplace stress is seen as a relatively new phenomenon. In reality, it has probably existed ever since prehistoric times, when early humans cooperated to hunt large animals.

Stress is different from a challenge. Challenge is a positive ingredient for healthy and productive work: it motivates staff to learn new skills and, when the challenge is met, everyone involved is able to relax and celebrate. Stress, however, is a harmful physical and emotional response when the challenge simply cannot be met, given the available resources. Symptoms of stress vary from relatively minor complaints including restless sleep and loss of appetite to severe anxiety and a complete breakdown of mental and physical health.

With the relentless drive for efficiency in today's commercial world, stress due to reorganization or the introduction of new technology is commonplace. Shareholder expectations in terms of improving revenue and profitability mean that directors have to 'squeeze the assets'. Within the services economy, staff account for the bulk of costs, so financial performance is linked directly to staff productivity.

Once seen as a boring and secure employer, the UK public sector is attracting bad publicity because of an apparent increase in workplace bullying. With the focus on effectiveness and reporting key performance indicators, public sector managers face challenging targets and are driving their staff hard. While most use a coaching approach, weaker managers resort to intimidation. The short-term consequences may be a small increase in productivity but at the expense in the medium term of staff losing their self-esteem and creativity. In the worst cases, litigation ensues – a traumatic process for the bully, the victim and the organization. The bully's reputation is usually destroyed, while a shadow of doubt is cast over the whole organization.

Various pieces of research have identified the following primary causes of occupational stress:

- *task design:* heavy workload, infrequent rest breaks, long work hours and shift work, and hectic and routine tasks that have little inherent meaning, do not utilize workers' skills and provide little sense of control;
- *management style:* lack of worker participation in decision making, poor communication in the organization, and lack of family-friendly policies;
- *interpersonal relationships:* poor social environment and lack of support or help from colleagues and supervisors;
- *work roles:* conflicting or uncertain job expectations, too much responsibility and too many 'hats' to wear;
- *career concerns:* job insecurity and lack of opportunity for growth, advancement or promotion, and rapid changes for which workers are unprepared;
- *environmental conditions:* unpleasant or dangerous physical conditions such as crowding, noise, air pollution or ergonomic problems.

High stress levels have been shown to reduce productivity and creativity and to increase costs in terms of absenteeism, litigation and staff turnover. There is no simple model for measuring the level of stress in an organization and changing it to achieve an optimum level.

As a general rule, organizations should start by performing analysis to establish whether there is a problem and, if there is, how big it is. Group discussions among managers and staff can provide invaluable information, to be followed by wider staff surveys. The main outcome should be a clear picture showing the high-stress points within the organization and their root causes.

The next stage is clearly to address the root causes. Some may be quick and easy to deal with (better communication), while others may take many months (redesign of a core process).

Finally, an appraisal should be carried out to establish whether the change has been effective in terms of reducing stress levels, but also in improving the effectiveness of that part of the organization.

Employment: legal overview

James Taylor, Simmons & Simmons

There is a large body of employment legislation, some of which, in particular several Acts relating to discrimination, has been in existence for many years and covers a broad range of issues that can be considered to be part of the sustainability debate. Employment law is a specialist area in its own right, but a few issues that touch upon the sustainability of an enterprise are mentioned here.

The Public Interest Disclosure Act 1998 came into force in July 1999. Under this Act, in provisions often referred to as 'whistleblower' protection provisions, a worker can disclose certain information about a company and obtain protection in relation to that disclosure. Qualifying disclosures include disclosures of any information that, in the reasonable belief of the worker, tends to show that the environment has been, is being or is likely to be damaged or that the health and safety of any individual has been, is being or is likely to be endangered.

Another developing area of employment law is workplace stress. The legislation addressing this issue overlaps with health and safety legislation, but includes measures such as the Working Time Regulations 1998, which (amongst other provisions) limit the number of hours that a worker can work in a week. Although workers can currently 'opt out' of the application of these regulations, employers should consider the possible effect on stress levels in their workforce of routinely requiring workers to work hours in excess of those provided for in the regulations.

The Working Time Directive (93/104/EC), for which the Working Time Regulations 1998 were implemented, is an ongoing legal issue for the UK, in part because of the fact that the UK currently permits employees to opt out of the 48-hour maximum working week. There is growing pressure to get rid of the opt-out clause, which culminated in a vote in favour of scrapping the provision when the issue came before MEPs in May 2005. The Council of Ministers has yet to approve the corresponding measure, which was mothballed during the UK's presidency of the EU in the latter half of 2005, and it remains to be seen whether the UK will be entitled to keep its opt-out.

There have been a number of cases that provide further guidance on the principles underlying an employer's liability for stress suffered by employees. In addition, the Health and Safety Executive is promoting management standards to address stress, and it is possible that such voluntary standards could become mandatory when seen in the context of wider health and safety duties.

The EU Equal Treatment Directive (2000/78/EC), which establishes a general framework for equality of treatment in employment on the grounds of age, disability, religion or belief and sexual orientation, came into force in 2000. Implementation of the directive was required by 2003, although member states were granted an additional three years beyond this date to implement the provisions on age and disability discrimination.

The UK has had the Sex Discrimination Act and Race Relations Act since 1975 and 1976 respectively and the Disability Discrimination Act since 1995. The UK has also prohibited discrimination on the grounds of religion, belief and sexual orientation since 2003. Consultation on draft age discrimination legislation took place throughout 2005, and regulations are scheduled to be laid before Parliament with a view to them entering into force in October 2006.

More to your
business
than meets the eye?

Same goes for us.

People. Training. HR Services.
Outsourcing. Consulting.
We're experts in our field.

We'll talk to you about your needs,
understand your business. Carry out a
full workforce analysis. Identify, measure
and deliver cost efficiencies and find
you the best people.

For all skills and levels visit
manpower.co.uk

What do you do?

Manpower

The changing world of work: an insight into work trends of 2016

Ruth Hounslow, Manpower UK

The situation

Today's world of work is unrecognizable from the workplace of only a few years ago. Employers and employees have embraced revolutionary communications advances, the introduction of flexible working arrangements, greater diversity in the workplace, and significant restructuring of working arrangements through outsourcing and offshoring.

Today, UK employers still face a number of challenges as they address the changing world of work – increasing business competition, a shortage of people with the right skills and the need to address employees' requirements for a work–life balance.

However, while all businesses need to manage today's changes, in order to be truly sustainable they must also prepare for the workplace of the future: how they will need to operate to remain competitive, the demands of a flexible workforce, the impact of technology and the skills they will need to maximize the opportunities ahead.

The Manpower report – *The Changing World of Work: An insight into work trends of 2016*

Recognizing that these changes will have a major impact on the workplace, Manpower commissioned a report in February 2006 to examine how employers and workers anticipate the world of work will change in the next 10 years. The report is based on independent research of 2,122 UK businesses conducted by National Opinion Polls (NOP) and separate research of 1,085 workers by Manpower.

The report reveals significant insights into the opinions of employers and employees on the workplace of the future and, in particular, very different expectations of the direction of future employment practice. Employers have a number of concerns not shared by their workers, with contrasting views around retirement age, productivity, skills development and IT.

Key findings of the report

The report shows that by 2016:

- 81 per cent of employees don't expect to work beyond the age of 65, but a majority of employers want them to do so (52 per cent);
- a clear majority of employers expect to measure their staff on productivity (68 per cent) and for those staff to develop more skills (72 per cent), but only a minority of employees believe this will be the case (22 per cent and 49 per cent respectively);
- the vast majority of employers think that IT will have a greater impact on work (84 per cent), compared with less than half of workers (43 per cent);
- homeworking will not significantly increase because of lack of demand from employers and employees (25 per cent and 15 per cent respectively);
- workers want to work flexibly (63 per cent) and employers recognize this as a significant benefit in terms of retention (84 per cent);
- employers believe more men will stay at home to bring up the family (41 per cent) and women will continue to break through the glass ceiling, playing an increasingly important role in management (83 per cent).

So the world of work is changing. Organizations today face a range of people issues: identifying the skills they need to succeed in the future; developing the right recruitment and retention programmes at every level of an organization; identifying the training needs of a workforce; looking outside a traditional labour pool to consider a truly diverse workforce including older workers and those from overseas; managing downsizing; and considering how best to outsource or offshore their operation.

Changing demographics – an ageing population and a declining birth rate – mean that the workforce is shrinking and will continue to do so, making finding people with the right skills hard. However, for those people with the right skills or who are willing to reskill, the opportunities are many and varied.

It will be the responsibility of employers, employees and governments to address the issues of education, training and skills development to equip people to succeed in the workplace of the future. It is particularly important for both employers and employees to recognize these changes and to be flexible in their approach to the needs of each other. It is vital that the differences in expectations of employers and employees identified in this research are resolved if we are to move forward into the future world of work successfully, productively and competitively.

Flexibility is key

Flexibility and skills development will be at the heart of the workplace of the future. Employers need people who have the right skills and a workforce that is flexible to compete in the global economy. Workers also want more flexibility – the opportunities to work the hours that best suit them and their other interests or needs, for example in balancing bringing up a family.

Employers need to look beyond their traditional sources of labour to help meet skills shortages. This includes engaging with older workers and mothers returning to work, and the use of migrant labour.

The challenge faced by business is ever present and growing. All organizations need to take urgent steps to see that they have in place the processes and systems to take account of this. Key will be to adopt these challenges as opportunities and to ensure that staff are aware of what will be required of them in the future.

The world of work is changing

The research indicates a high level of agreement between employers and workers that the world of work is changing. Overall, three-quarters of businesses in the UK (73 per cent) feel that the world of work is changing compared with 97 per cent of workers.

However, the perception of the speed of change differs markedly (see Figure 3.7.1), with 39 per cent of businesses stating that the world of work is changing at a faster pace than ever before, compared with 83 per cent of employees. Just 8 per cent of businesses and only 1 per cent of workers think the world of work is not changing at all.

The research also reveals that changes occurring in the world of work are shared by businesses irrespective of the sector in which they operate (see Figure 3.7.2): employers in the transport and communications and community and social sectors are amongst the most convinced that the world of work is changing (83 per cent and 75 per cent respectively). Those in the hotels and retail sector are the most sceptical about changes that are occurring in the modern workplace, but a clear majority believe it is changing (66 per cent overall).

The nature of jobs of the future

The nature of jobs and the ways in which people work will change noticeably over the next decade. Businesses are split equally as to how jobs will be affected (see Figure 3.7.3), with 48 per cent believing that the nature of jobs will have noticeably

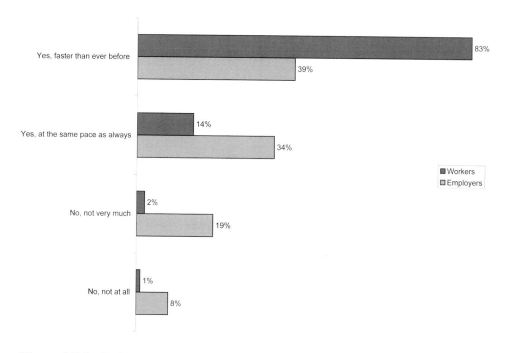

Figure 3.7.1   Is the world of work changing? (1)

changed. Amongst employees, only 9 per cent of workers believe their job will not have noticeably changed. However, whilst jobs are likely to have changed, workers do not believe their jobs will become obsolete.

How organizations and workers see the workplace changing

There is a clear disparity between businesses and employees in their perceptions of how the workplace will have changed in 10 years' time (see Figure 3.7.4). The majority of businesses agree that the workplace of the future will be an environment more influenced by technology, where staff will work later in life, where their workers will be increasingly measured on their output/productivity and workers will have developed more skills. However, in contrast, less than half of employees agree that any of these changes will affect how they do their job in 10 years' time.

Employers see output/productivity as a clear concern for the future. Over two-thirds (68 per cent) of businesses agree that in 10 years' time their staff will be increasingly measured on this. Workers, on the other hand, do not recognize this as so important – less than one-quarter (22 per cent) of employees believe this will be the case. Businesses need to set clear goals, objectives and direction to make clear to workers that productivity is key.

The majority of businesses believe that IT will have a greater impact upon how they operate in 10 years' time (84 per cent). However, about half that percentage of workers feel IT will impact on how they will work (43 per cent). Employees identify

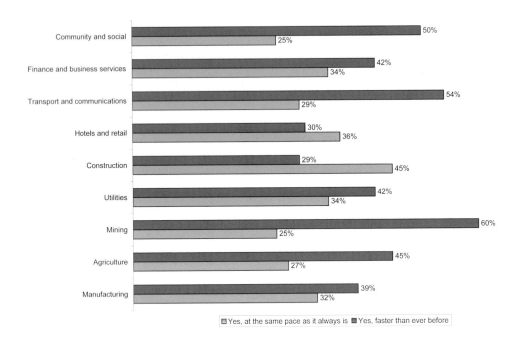

Figure 3.7.2 Is the world of work changing? (2)

skills development as the most likely change to the way in which they will work in the future (46 per cent); however, this sentiment falls significantly short of the view of businesses (72 per cent).

The impact of an ageing population looks set to create problems. There is a notable difference between employers and workers concerning the future age of the workplace: more than half of businesses (52 per cent) agree that they will want staff to work beyond the age of 65 – but just 19 per cent of employees say they will do this.

Engaging staff effectively: flexibility and gender in the workplace

A flexible workforce is of major importance for many businesses. Labour market flexibility will enable businesses to compete effectively in the UK and global marketplace. And in a changing work environment, employers must also recognize that workers want more control of how and when they work. This can cover such areas as variable hours, part-time working, homeworking, job sharing or working compressed working weeks.

Businesses understand that adopting flexible working practices is of significant benefit to attracting and managing the workforce (see Figure 3.7.5). Businesses believe that a flexible approach to work will be a major driver in improving staff retention (84 per cent) and that the majority believe their workers will work more flexibly in 2016 (70 per cent). At the same time, 63 per cent of employees want to make use of flexible working hours in the future.

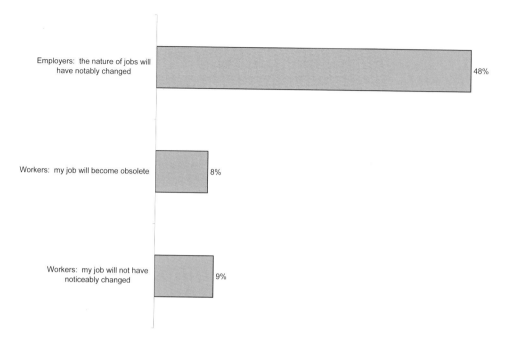

Figure 3.7.3   Nature of jobs of the future

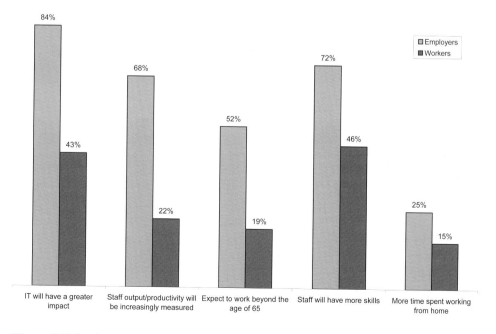

Figure 3.7.4   Agreement about changes in the workplace

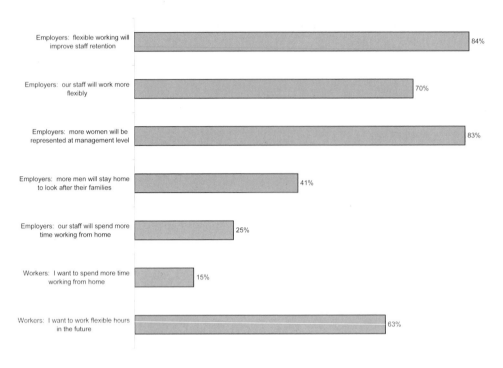

Figure 3.7.5   Attitudes to flexible hours and working from home

Interestingly, neither employers nor workers expect a marked increase in homework-ing: 25 per cent of employers believe their staff will spend more time working from home and 15 per cent of workers believe they will do likewise.

At the same time, employers recognize that there is a shift in the role men and women play in the workforce. The future workplace looks set to be one where women play a greater role than today – 83 per cent of businesses believe women will be more represented at management level in 10 years' time. And, at the same time, men will increasingly take on a role in bringing up a family, with 41 per cent of employers believing more men will choose to stay at home to do this.

Conclusions

The workplace of 10 years' time will have changed noticeably. IT will play a greater role; generally the workforce will be older; people will have developed more skills; there will be an increased focus on productivity; flexibility will increasingly be the norm; women will take more management positions; men will play a larger role in raising children.

Yet at the same time there are a number of discrepancies between the views of employers and workers and the expectations each have. In many cases, the views of employers are not shared to the same extent by workers. Nowhere is this clearer than when considering at what age people will stop working: older workers have a wealth of experience and, whilst more employers expect that those over the age of 65 will still be working, very few workers want to continue working when they reach that point.

Flexibility will be at the heart of the workplace of the future – a flexible approach to how an employer manages its workforce to meet the challenges of a competitive marketplace and the need to recognize the desires of employees to have more control over how and when they work. A very real deliverable is for employers to address the skills shortage by taking a flexible approach – looking beyond their traditional labour pool or providing flexible working practices that allow mothers to work part time.

It will be important for workers to understand the challenges businesses will face but also for employers to recognize the needs of employees. The challenge for employers and employees is how to anticipate the issues and opportunities the changing world of work presents. It is not enough to ignore these or pay lip service to them – they must be planned for and proactive steps taken to ensure the needs of all parties can be included where possible.

Recognizing that the world of work is changing is of crucial importance. But companies also need to take a sustainable approach to their working practices by embracing such issues as diversity and flexibility. It is those companies that take such an enlightened approach that will be the ones that succeed in the workplace of tomorrow.

4

Business and the community

CALVERTS

Founded in 1977, Calverts is a one-stop communications design and printing company. It is 100% employee-owned, and serves client organisations across the private, public and voluntary sectors.

A socially responsible firm and a class leader in sustainable design and print, Calverts holds the GreenMark and Inner City 100 awards, and is a level B1 signatory to the London Green Procurement Code.

Calverts works with agencies, consultancies and end-user clients to improve the social and environmental impacts of their print communications.

Services
- Professional graphic and publications design
- Illustration, photography, editing and copywriting
- Reprographics
- High quality colour litho printing
- Wide format and digital printing
- Full range of print finishes and binding styles
- Print mailing and UK or worldwide distribution
- Free samples, dummies and advice service

Products
- Newsletters and magazines
- Catalogues and brochures
- Flyers, leaflets and posters
- Business stationery
- Folders, packs and binders
- Display and point-of-sale materials
- Annual reports and books
- Full range of recycled and FSC accredited papers

Calverts environmental statement, client list and portfolio are available at www.calverts.coop

Calverts
9-10 The Oval, London E2 9DT
T: 020 7739 1474
F: 020 7739 0881
E: info@calverts.coop
www.calverts.coop

Calverts North Star Press Ltd is registered under the Industrial & Provident Societies Act 1965, Reg No 21946R

Marketing and consumption: legal overview

James Taylor, Simmons & Simmons

Sustainable consumption is one of the fastest-developing themes in the sustainability framework, and sustainable consumption and production (SCP) is one of the four priority areas for UK action set out in the new sustainable development strategy, *Securing the Future*, published in March 2005, which takes forward the *Changing Patterns* paper published in 2003. The new strategy focuses on encouraging better products and services (which reduce the environmental impacts from the use of energy, resources or hazardous substances); cleaner, more efficient production processes (which strengthen competitiveness); and shifts in consumption towards goods and services with lower impacts. One of the key tools is the development of a set of SCP indicators to monitor the extent to which the UK is 'decoupling' the link between increasing economic growth and environmental damage.

At European level, Integrated Product Policy (IPP) was first debated in 1998, and September 2003 saw the Commission releasing a Communication to the Council and the European Parliament on IPP, 'Building on environmental life-cycle thinking'. The Communication outlines the strategy for reducing the environmental impact caused by products, and implementation actions include 'IPP regular meetings' with member states, countries from the European Economic Area and stakeholders. The Commission is carrying out two pilot projects to demonstrate how IPP can work in practice, on mobile phones (with Nokia) and on a teak garden chair (with Carrefour). These projects began in mid-June 2004 and will end in 2006. In 2004 the Commission also launched a programme with the purpose of identifying products with the greatest potential for environmental improvement from a life-cycle perspective, which is intended to conclude by 2007.

Brand integrity in the sustainable enterprise

Ian Bretman, The Fairtrade Foundation

The increasing attention given to sustainability issues, whether by investors, consumers or wider society through government and the media, creates a new set of challenges for brand management. There are almost as many approaches to branding as there are brand names in the market and it is not the intention of this chapter to try to summarize them, but the trend for brands to be more than just a marketing tool is undeniable. The contemporary brand is increasingly the framework, usually defined through a set of explicit or implicit values, through which relationships within and without the organization are managed in order to pursue the organization's mission. The brand therefore defines the way that people think and feel about your company and its products or services. Indeed, Richard Branson says that 'It is feelings – and feelings alone – that account for the success of the Virgin brand in all its myriad forms.'

In an increasingly busy and complex world in which we all have more choice than ever, but less time in which to exercise it, we usually rely on our feelings to summarize our view of a particular product from among the hundreds available to us. Those feelings might be suggested through advertising (think Volvo and safety or Volkswagen and reliability) but advertising is only effective if it reflects people's experience of the brand. In other words, your brand is what a customer thinks about you at least as much as the image you try to convey, and so branding is, more than anything, about establishing and retaining the trust of consumers in your company. It's that trust that enables Virgin to sell us everything from flights to mobile phones and from cars to drinks; and it's trust that has enabled Tesco to be more than just a grocer and to account for over 12 per cent of all retail spending in Britain. Rita Clifton, chair of Interbrand, has said that 'Public relations for brands will succeed only if they are based on the brand promise and the internal reality of the company. People have become increasingly sceptical and, in a 24-hour news culture, organizations have nowhere to hide, either inside or outside.'

If people trust your company and your brand then they clearly have expectations of you – and these are in a different realm from the expectations they have of your core business, which you can identify, evaluate and measure your performance against. If you're taking the trouble to read this book then you probably aim to meet, or more likely exceed, those expectations. But how do you know what people expect of you in terms of sustainability? And how can you ensure that – at the very least – your company is not associated with practices that if exposed, now or in the future, could result in damage to your brand?

This is the question that has tended to be the starting point for most corporate social responsibility initiatives. As a first step, scrutiny of internal policies and operations is essential, but, in today's business environment in which companies outsource many of their non-core activities, consideration of supply chains is also important, as companies can be held accountable for the activities of their suppliers. This is far more complex, especially when production is outsourced to developing countries. Even in Britain where there is a regulatory framework for employment conditions we have seen incidents like the deaths in February 2004 of 18 Chinese workers while picking cockles in Morecambe Bay.

Companies have responded to the need for closer control of supply chain management by developing codes of conduct for their own operations and those of their suppliers. In Britain, the Ethical Trading Initiative (ETI) was set up in 1998 as an alliance of companies, NGOs and trade unions to share learning on the implementation of codes relating to working conditions across corporate supply chains. The ETI Base Code, which provides a template of minimum provisions based on the established conventions of the International Labour Organization, covers areas such as the avoidance of forced, bonded or child labour, freedom of association, safe working conditions, limits on working hours, the payment of living wages and the avoidance of discrimination and harsh treatment. Thirty-seven companies are currently members of ETI, including the market leaders in food, clothing and houseware retailing, many of their largest suppliers and a number of leading international brands such as Levi Strauss, Gap and Chiquita.

Although work in this area is at an early stage and there is still a great deal to do, it has enabled companies to identify areas of good practice and those that need to be improved. It has also taken place quietly and with little communication to consumers, as companies recognize that they are working towards the expectations of the market. Companies that aim for excellence in their business relationships are therefore looking at how they manage the impact of their business on issues like human rights and the environment in a way that will exceed society's expectations of them. To quote Rita Clifton of Interbrand again: 'Corporate social responsibility should be about genuinely solving problems, not just about brand reputation management.'

Moreover, this is a dynamic environment – society's expectations are changing over time. Two hundred years ago, even after 30 years of campaigning by reformers, most people in this country thought that slavery was bad, but inevitable. Similarly, campaigns to abolish child labour in Britain started in the 1820s with laws proposed by the Earl of Shaftesbury but it took over 70 years until legislation looked anything like its current form. For much of that period, the business and investment communities opposed such progressive moves, seemingly stuck in a mindset that any increase in costs would be disastrous. In the 1840s, the textile manufacturer Samuel Courtauld stated that 'Legislative interference in the arrangement and conduct of business is always injurious, tending to check improvement and to increase the cost of production.' However, when attitudes changed, the law changed with them, and business adapted – as it always has done.

Today, we are seeing increasingly popular movements for further improvements in social and environmental standards. The Make Poverty History campaign in 2005, and the massive events leading up to that year's G8 summit in Gleneagles, focused on increased debt relief, better and more aid and improved terms of trade for the poorest countries of the world. It did not, and was never intended to, eliminate poverty in one year. But it does seem to have changed attitudes, especially among young people, about global poverty from the position of it being bad but inevitable, to a growing awareness that the problem can – and therefore should – be resolved.

One of the most visible aspects of this changing attitude can be seen in the growing sales of Fairtrade products in Britain and around the world. Fairtrade standards aim to improve the position of marginalized and disadvantaged farmers and workers in the developing world, and to help them compete more effectively in international markets. Crucially, Fairtrade products mean that the producers have been paid a sustainable price for their products that includes a premium for investment in social or economic improvements. Britain's FAIRTRADE Mark was launched in 1994 and currently certifies over 1,500 product lines made with or from tea, coffee, cocoa, sugar, honey and a wide range of fruits. In recent years, Fairtrade has moved into non-food products such as flowers and cotton. Companies that don't trade in these products directly are also getting involved by sourcing their consumable supplies as Fairtrade certified as part of their wider CSR policies.

Britain's Fairtrade Foundation is one of 20 national organizations across Europe, North America, Japan and Australia that certify products to common standards set by Fairtrade Labelling Organizations International. This body now certifies over 550 producer organizations – either small farmer associations or democratic worker groups – in over 50 countries. It's estimated that Fairtrade is making a difference to the lives of over 1 million farmers and workers – probably 5 million people when family members are included – even though it accounts for a very small proportion of global trade in the commodities it certifies.

Sales of Fairtrade products in Britain have been rising by 40 per cent per annum over the past four years and hit an annual rate of £200 million at the start of 2006. More and more consumers are becoming aware of the Mark – 52 per cent of the UK population according to a MORI survey in May 2005. The same survey also found that 86 per cent of people who buy Fairtrade products rate the independent guarantee offered by the FAIRTRADE Mark as either 'very' or 'quite' important. Yet some companies are wary of using an external label, preferring to rely on consumer trust in their own brand, although the success of companies such as Cafédirect, Clipper, Green & Black's and Percol, which have built strong brand reputations in their own right through a long association with the FAIRTRADE Mark, demonstrates that these concerns are misplaced.

Among retailers, the Co-op has also carved out a strong niche in 'responsible retailing', with Fairtrade at the heart of this strategy. For more than two years all Co-op brand coffee and chocolate bars have been Fairtrade certified, and Co-op stores sell the largest range of Fairtrade products of any national retailer. A survey by the UK trade magazine *The Grocer* in 2005 found that the public recognized this as a distinct point of difference for the Co-op. Many other companies, such as AMT Coffee and Virgin Trains, are recognizing the trend in Fairtrade by converting all their beverages to the standard certified by the FAIRTRADE Mark, rather than just offering it as an alternative choice. They have been joined by Marks & Spencer, which has recently announced that all its coffees and teas will be Fairtrade certified – and, since it only sells own-brand products, this will become the universal standard in its shops. All of these companies are moving to position their business to the point that they feel is appropriate for their brands in relation to where they expect consumer expectations to be in the foreseeable future.

From a very small niche, Fairtrade has become a small but significant part of the mainstream retail market in Britain, securing a market share of around 5 per cent in coffee (with nearly 20 per cent in the premium roast and ground sector) and 8 per cent in bananas. More importantly, it is backed by what the *Guardian* described as 'one of the fastest-growing grass-roots social movements in Britain', as organizations such as local authorities, churches and other places of worship, schools, universities and workplaces all help to embed Fairtrade into their local communities. There are now over 180 Fairtrade towns and cities around Britain, awarded the title after meeting defined goals for establishing awareness and support in their areas.

The Fairtrade Foundation's experience over the past 10 years suggests that an increasing number of companies would like to do more to promote sustainable development because they see it as a better way of doing business for its own sake and not just to respond to consumer interest. There is therefore a further challenge in securing the sustainability of this process itself and to ensure that, in an increasingly sceptical world, we do not promise more than we can deliver in the pursuit of marketing advantage. In this respect, independent, standards-based certification labels like the FAIRTRADE Mark can be a valuable tool for brand integrity, as well as enabling business to play its part in resolving some of the biggest challenges facing our society in the 21st century.

Green labelling

Nick Cliffe, Forest Stewardship Council

More and more products now carry information about their environmental profile, whether it's regarding their potential for recycling, the lack of toxic substances used in their manufacture or how the impact of their production on the environment is less than that of other, competitor products. Though it is useful to consumers, there is not yet much legal requirement to provide this information, so why are so many companies seeking to offer this kind of information to consumers? There are several reasons why you may wish to make a green claim about your company's products:

- To inform consumers of the environmental benefits of your product. Consumer interest in environmental issues is increasing, and the percentage of consumers who weigh the environmental cost of what they buy is growing steadily.
- Environmental labels are a useful tool for demonstrating your corporate social responsibility to customers, partners and other regulators.
- They help raise awareness of issues that are important to your sector.
- They help to improve product standards, and keeping a careful eye on the environmental profile of your product range may help you to avoid problems as new environmental legislation or labelling requirements are introduced.

There are two ways to make an environmental claim: it can be self-declared or done via an existing environmental labelling or declaration scheme.

Self-declared environmental claims

A self-declared environmental claim is considered to be any statement, symbol or graphic that refers to any environmental aspect of a product, component of a product or packaging. Such a claim can appear on the product or packaging itself, or on any associated marketing materials.

Before considering making such a claim, you should establish whether your product is the subject of legal labelling requirements. These are not common, but there are some – such as the European Energy Label (see page 128). Mandatory requirements also exist for the food and drink and the pharmaceutical sectors, and where necessary you should seek detailed advice from the appropriate trade association or your local trading standards officer. For more information, see www.tradingstandards.gov.uk.

There are two references that should guide the process of making self-declared environmental claims in the United Kingdom: ISO 14021 (developed by the International Organization for Standardization) and the Green Claims Code (published by the Department for Environment, Food and Rural Affairs (Defra) and the Department of Trade and Industry (DTI)). The Green Claims Code is a user-friendly introduction to ISO 14021 and provides guidance on best practice. Copies can be obtained from Defra. Defra also publishes specific guidance for several sectors, such as growing media, greetings cards, decorative coatings, cleaning products and aerosols. For more information, see www.defra.gov.uk/environment/consumerprod.

Generally speaking, there are three things you need to take account of when making a self-declared environmental claim:

■ content;
■ presentation;
■ assurance of accuracy.

Content

Any claim should be accurate and truthful. Avoid making claims that, while true, are not particularly relevant. Don't make multiple claims about one environmental benefit of the product using different wordings. You should also ensure that any claim is relevant to that particular product. Do not, for example, make a claim about the packaging of a product that might be interpreted as being a claim about the product itself. A misinterpretation of this kind is often possible when the Möbius loop (see page 126) is used to indicate recycled content or recyclability. It is also important to ensure that you regularly review any claim you are making to ensure it is still accurate.

Your claim should also be specific and unambiguous. Descriptions such as 'environmentally friendly' are essentially meaningless, and claims such as this have, in the past, discredited green claims. You should state a specific benefit (such as the absence of a previously used toxic substance in the product) or make a clear positive comparison with alternatives to the product. Note that when making comparisons it is important to have hard data to back up your claims.

Presentation

Once you have developed a claim that is accurate, relevant and unambiguous, it is important to present it clearly. Avoid using small print or language that may exaggerate the nature of the claim. Remember too that many consumers may lack in-depth knowledge of technical terms, so use plain English wherever possible.

A common way to communicate information is graphically through the use of symbols or icons. If you decide to do this, make sure the meaning is clear, and add supporting statements if required.

Accuracy

When you are making a self-declared environmental claim, there is no need to seek third-party verification, but you must be able to substantiate the claim and provide this supporting information to anyone who requests it. Bear in mind that a false claim could result in prosecution by trading standards authorities. Ensure that any claim you make has been tested and verified. Also, be wary of making a claim that may require you to reveal sensitive commercial information if you are asked to verify its accuracy.

Always keep appropriate records of testing, as this is particularly important if you are making a comparative claim, especially against a competitor product. In this instance you may wish to consider getting an independent organization to carry out the work. You should keep all information relevant to a claim for the entire lifetime of the product.

The alternative to making a self-declared environmental claim is another method of demonstrating the environmental benefits of your products – using existing labelling schemes that offer independent, third-party verification. The next section looks at these.

Existing labelling schemes

There are many benefits to using existing labelling schemes. Most obviously, they provide a ready-made system, thus saving you time in quantifying the environmental costs inherent to your particular business. By researching and selecting a suitable and respected labelling system that already exists for your sector, you in effect receive a ready-made checklist to ensure that your product meets a suitable environmental standard. The certification process will most likely take care of all requirements related to accuracy and verification, and regular audits will ensure that your claim is always up to date.

Many of these schemes also offer you pre-existing consumer awareness. Some carry out a great deal of direct marketing to customers, both business and consumer, informing them directly of the environmental benefits of products that meet their criteria. The scheme may also offer you free entry in catalogues or websites that list products certified under the scheme. Some schemes may even host trade and consumer shows where you can promote your products directly to target markets, and have a system for developing market linkages, thereby helping you find new markets for your products.

These schemes provide independent assurance for your customers. Most are operated on a not-for-profit basis and so are viewed as more trustworthy than a commercial concern. Some are even endorsed by major environmental charities, such as Greenpeace, Friends of the Earth and WWF.

A reverse benefit of such schemes is that they can assist in your own purchasing: many of these schemes operate a chain-of-custody system to track goods from source to consumer. By seeking suppliers already certified under a particular scheme, you can become another link in the chain, providing you with a ready-made buyer's specification.

But bear in mind that most of these schemes will carry a cost, both in terms of adjusting your operations to meet the criteria and for any auditing that gaining certification entails. You should explore the costs of becoming certified under any scheme carefully and, where there are several relevant schemes (or auditors that offer the same form of certification), compare costs.

There are many existing labelling schemes. Some are sector- or issue-specific, whereas others are more general. In all cases you should select the scheme that offers the best fit with your company activity. When you have selected a scheme, the first step is to contact those running it and ascertain what the procedure is for gaining the use of the mark. In many cases this will require an independent audit and also changes to your systems and supply chains, so careful planning and budgeting are strongly advised. Note also that many schemes may require you to use accredited certifiers for auditing, in which case it's important to shop around to get the best deal.

In addition to gaining use of an appropriate mark, you may also need to consider communicating to your customers what the mark is and what it represents.

Möbius loop

The Möbius loop is used throughout the world to denote goods that are either re-cyclable or contain recycled content. It is both the most widely used and the most widely recognized of green labels. There are many versions of the logo in use, but they all share the same basic structure of three arrows (representing the three stages of recycling: collection, reprocessing and resale). Where a percentage appears within the loop, it indicates the percentage of recycled content. If no percentage appears, this indicates that the product itself is recyclable. Full guidelines on the use of the loop are given in ISO 14020.

EU Ecolabel

The European Ecolabel is an official EU mark awarded to products with the highest environmental performance in the marketplace. The system was developed by the European Commission and is managed in the United Kingdom by Defra. The environmental impact of the product throughout its entire life cycle must be assessed and independently certified in order to use the mark. There are currently 21 product

Textiles	Paper (copying and graphic)	Paper (tissue)
All-purpose cleaners	Soil improvers	Footwear
Personal computers	Portable computers	Televisions
Refrigerators	Tourist accommodation	Mattresses
Detergents (dishwashers)	Detergents (laundry)	Detergents (hand washing)
Indoor paint and varnish	Hard floor coverings	Washing machines
Light bulbs	Dishwashers	Vacuum cleaners

Figure 4.3.1   Product groups covered by the European Ecolabel

groups covered by the system, as shown in Figure 4.3.1. For more information, see www.europa.eu.int/comm/environment/ecolabel.

Green Dot (der Grüne Punkt)

The Green Dot is a system for packaging that indicates that the company has paid a financial contribution to a packaging recovery company within the country of origin. It is not currently in operation within the United Kingdom, which instead has packaging regulations based on a system of packaging waste recovery notes (PRNs). The Green Dot system is used within many EU states, including Austria, Belgium, France, Germany, the Republic of Ireland, Luxembourg, Portugal, Spain and Sweden. If your company operates in these countries, your operation may be eligible for participation in the scheme. For more information, see www.green-dot.com.

Fairtrade

The FAIRTRADE Mark on a product demonstrates that the product has met the international Fairtrade standards, which guarantee that producers in developing countries receive a fair price that covers costs and provides a premium for producers to invest in their communities: clean water, health care, education and the environment.

The FAIRTRADE Mark is widely recognized, and consumer demand for Fairtrade products is growing. In addition, the mark is being heavily promoted by participating companies as well as the Fairtrade organization itself. Currently, the majority of

Fairtrade products are food or beverages, but this is beginning to change, and any company sourcing materials from developing countries can apply to use the mark. For more information, see www.fairtrade.org.uk.

Marine Stewardship Council

The Marine Stewardship Council certifies products of fishing, based on an internationally recognized environmental standard for well-managed fisheries. For more information, see www.msc.org.

Forest Stewardship Council

The Forest Stewardship Council operates a system for the certification of well-managed woodlands according to strict environmental, social and economic standards. There is also a chain-of-custody system for tracking timber from these forests to final products. Certification is carried out by independent, third-party auditors and, if the appropriate standard is met, the FSC logo may be shown on the product. Certification is available for all timber and timber fibre products, including paper and recycled timber. For more information, see www.fsc-uk.org.

Leaf Marque

The Leaf Marque system operates on the basis of linking the environment and farming. Products carrying the Leaf Marque are produced by farmers who have demonstrated their commitment to improving the environment for the benefit of both wildlife and the countryside. For more information, see www.leafmarque.com.

Organic food (various)

There are many labels that indicate that a food product is organically produced. Organic farming in Europe is governed by EC regulation 2092/1991 and requires certification by an accredited organization. Within the United Kingdom, the body responsible for implementing this is the United Kingdom Register of Organic Food Standards (UKROFS). This body accredits independent organizations to inspect and certify farms and other producers and their products as organic.

There are many such independent organizations within the United Kingdom. A full list is available from Defra at http://www.defra.gov.uk/farm/organic/certbodies/approved.htm.

Energy

There are several schemes applicable to electronic appliances and their energy profile.

European Energy Label

All European manufacturers and retailers are required by law to inform consumers of the energy efficiency of many types of appliances, particularly white goods. The

European Energy Label rates appliances from A (most efficient) to G (least efficient). For more information, see www.mtprog.com.

Energy efficiency recommended

The Energy Saving Trust awards products with high energy efficiency. Various categories of appliance are eligible to be considered for the award, including white goods, light bulbs and fittings, loft insulation, cavity wall insulation and draught-proofing. For more information, see http://www.est.org.uk/.

Energy Star

Energy Star is a voluntary labelling system that operates across the world. Its use is controlled by an agreement between the United States and the European Union. It indicates that the energy consumption of a product is below an agreed level when in stand-by mode. Various products are eligible for the scheme, including computers, monitors, printers and fax machines. For more information, see www.energystar.gov.

Corporate responsibility and innovation

John Sabapathy, AccountAbility

Innovating through corporate responsibility: what Milton Friedman meant to say

We all know the Milton Friedman quotation: 'The business of business is society.' At least, that's what he should have said. Any business not attuned to its customers, the people around whom it operates, the governments that regulate it, the employees that power it and the environmental resources that sustain it will in the end fail to do business. Any business that does these things does business, at least in democratic markets. And if a business does these things, it understands what it means to operate responsively to the needs and preferences of its stakeholders – understands, that is to say, corporate responsibility.

The trick, as always, is to align what the company does with the most important of its social, environmental and economic impacts on society. But much of the controversy surrounding the supposed 'uncompetitiveness' of corporate responsibility has arisen as a downside from understandable and valuable initiatives to define that black box labelled 'corporate responsibility'. Problems only emerge if broad-brush approaches to corporate responsibility are applied without consideration for the specific sustainability challenges and opportunities any given company faces. Clearly, just as all businesses have their own business model, so too do they need their own model to make corporate responsibility beneficial rather than irrelevant.

A recent Europe-wide survey of business leaders found that 76 per cent of them believe that 'responsible business practice can promote innovation and creativity within the organization'. Specifically, 79 per cent agreed that 'responsible business practice offers us an opportunity to learn from outside the organization', while 83 per cent agreed that it also 'allows us to learn more about our marketplace'.

This is, as it were, the bad news. The good news is that increasing numbers of companies are making success stories from corporate responsibility strategies that balance the broad-brush with the bespoke. We know that innovation drives business success. The more that companies are able to derive value from unique products and processes, the stronger their basis of competitive advantage. Corporate innovation at its best is individual. Corporate responsibility can help drive innovation.

This breaks down in a number of ways. Companies' experience shows that corporate responsibility – when it is aligned to companies' core drivers, impacts and business – can:

■　help companies understand the needs and concerns of their stakeholders;
■　provide insights into customer concerns and new market opportunities;
■　give forewarnings of emerging consumer trends and expectations;
■　make direct links through to significant communities that a company sites with, supplies, sells to and employs.

The building blocks to this sort of community-enabled innovation can be set out and illustrated quite simply by four practical propositions.

Community-enabled innovation: practical propositions

1. *Community engagement can enable business innovation.* Corporate experience shows that community engagement can enable business innovation when it is geared towards generating new insights into companies' interaction with society. Benefiting in this way requires recognition that applying business skills to important social and environmental issues can result in new insights and innovations. Management strategies are only built around new insights and returns, which is a significant factor in successfully creating community-enabled innovation.

> Dow Chemicals has been able to identify a wide range of product and process innovations through its Responsible Care Awards scheme, which encourages staff to develop and pilot sustainability schemes with a range of civil-society partners. More broadly, a range of knowledge management systems within Dow encourages local business units to feed insights and views of local environmental and community groups into its decision-making processes.

2. *Community-enabled innovation adds most value when it is part and parcel of a company's product and management processes.* Often, the limited business

benefit and social impact from corporate responsibility programmes arise from a disconnection between core business and the corporate responsibility activity itself. This is one of the drawbacks of many classic forms of corporate philanthropy that indirectly benefit the business by creating associations in the minds of customers or others between 'good works' and the company. To gain real benefits, the company must engage material social or environmental issues with its core competencies and products.

> Travelers Property Casualty has worked with the National Insurance Task Force coalition and community-based non-governmental organizations (NGOs) both to increase the affordability and quality of insurance available in inner-city areas and to raise low-income homeowners' awareness of home hazards and their ability to make their homes safer. Drawing on its own core competency – a knowledge of hazards in the home and how to protect against them – Travelers has been able to help make neighbourhoods safer and to improve the market for home ownership insurances.

3. *Responsiveness to relevant community needs is a prerequisite of community-enabled innovation.* Where a community's own needs are not addressed through corporate engagement, the opportunities for community-enabled innovation will be wasted. The problem has been in putting this theory into practice. Responsiveness to signals in the market is a skill that business managers identify as one of the keys to innovation. In the same way, the art of community-enabled innovation lies in the quality of a company's response to stakeholders' needs. It is only by being responsive that companies are testing the boundaries of learning, and creating new solutions within dynamic market environments. Without a willingness to handle the challenges that communities face, companies cannot create the reciprocity that will encourage the community constructively to engage with them.

> Tesco's strategic innovation of store development in low- to moderate-income inner-city areas has been highly successful United Kingdom-wide. Enabled by responsive engagement with the transport, childcare and training needs of potential employees, the 'regeneration partnerships' have led to the creation of 12 stores in urban areas previously deemed too difficult to serve and invest in. Altering existing processes to accommodate community needs and partnering with local community groups and employment services was critical in getting to the heart of the conditions that would determine the stores' success.

4. *Community-enabled innovation can increase the accountability of the company to key stakeholders – but not always.* Accountability has become an important driver

in defining responsible business strategies. In this regard, part of the attractiveness of community-enabled innovation is that it is manageable and focused. It is therefore relatively easy for a company to be accountable to a community for the duration of a project or partnership. However, it is quite a different proposition to extend and embed a partnership-specific approach to accountability within production and management processes. For example, institutional initiatives within the field of supply chain labour standards that have developed as corporate, NGO and (sometimes) union partnerships have all had to demonstrate to whom they are ultimately accountable and therefore whether they ultimately justify the civil-society legitimacy they seek. What is clear is that the longer the partnership the more critical it is to establish accountability mechanisms that structure the terms of a company's relationship with a particular community. Ultimately, accountability to communities helps companies build the credibility and licence to operate, irrespective of what they sell or how they sell it.

> Suez, for example, has developed new forms of collaboration with low-income groups in Central America in order to deliver water projects effectively in newly privatized areas. The result of an acknowledgement that long-term approaches to partnerships are required for such infrastructure investment, these partnerships embody new strategies for engaging with grass-roots communities whose needs have not always been incorporated into such development projects. In addition, Suez has developed the Observatoire Sociale Mondiale (OSI), a bespoke internal advisory group convening key civil-society groups in order to increase the company's learning about emerging issues and concerns.

Reasons why there is not more community-enabled innovation

Besides the fact that companies may not have thought about the potential opportunities of community-enabled innovation, our research suggests two fundamental reasons.

The first is that community-enabled innovation is unlikely to occur unless the expectations, implications and required resources are factored in from the start. If companies don't expect to gain innovation from their engagement with communities, they won't spend much time looking for it and they are unlikely to find it. Why don't businesses expect to find community-enabled innovation? Leadership within a company may be insufficiently convinced about its potential business value. Business executives may have watched the varying financial fortunes of highly branded 'responsible' companies such as the Body Shop, Iceland or Ben & Jerry's and concluded that such approaches could not function as a long-term business strategy. They may have looked at the uptake of 'sustainability reporting' among many of the world's leading companies and not seen the findings of such reports filtering back into the decision-making processes at the very top.

One of the core barriers has in fact been created by a one-size-fits-all approach to 'selling' the business case for corporate responsibility. As the cases show, however, a fundamental characteristic of all the community-enabled innovation approaches is an individually designed response to idiosyncratic market conditions – social and environmental, as well as economic. In no area of business would companies expect to gain performance improvements by simply applying generic principles, and corporate responsibility is no different. Some of the most interesting recent legislation (such as the United Kingdom's draft Operating and Financial Review) acknowledges precisely this through its emphasis on companies' own identification of what are the relevant and material sustainable issues facing them.

The second reason has less to do with problems of perception and expectation than with the fact that not all companies are necessarily in a position to produce community-enabled innovation. There are reasons why BP and Novo A/S have generated innovation through community engagement, while many of their sector peers have not. The question then becomes 'How does a company identify the basis on which it can individually innovate in this area?'

Analysing companies' experience in this regard throws up four key strategic factors that determine the extent to which a company is likely to be able to develop community-enabled innovation successfully.

Community-enabled innovation: strategic factors

1. *The company responds to challenges from community groups as an opportunity for engagement and dialogue with stakeholders.*

   Many of the companies we engaged with as leaders in this field have been at the centre of critical debates about their social, environmental and economic impact. In the case of Tesco and other UK supermarkets, the debate has been about the impact of supermarkets on town centres and smaller high street retailers. Dow and other chemical companies have been drawn into discussions concerning the chemical industry's responsibility for accidental emissions.

   The existence (often in the media) of such debates is a highly effective means of linking core activities with corporate responsibility strategies and encouraging those at the top to adopt strategies of engagement with such issues. Similarly, it is often harder for companies that have not experienced crises, and the impetus for change they can create, to find effective triggers for engagement within the company.

   While a crisis can help focus management's attention on communities, it is not the presence or absence of a crisis that determines whether or not a company can innovate through community engagement. Rather, it is whether the company responds by engagement and dialogue or by defensiveness and distancing. Companies that respond to challenges with vigorous legal and public relations counter-attacks, rather than dialogue, are unlikely to generate innovation in the process.

   Action implication: Advocates within companies should identify whether the willingness to embrace dialogue in response to challenges is likely to tip corporate reaction to challenges towards community-enabled innovation or whether the barriers are likely to prove too high.

2. *The company's core skills in innovating are in areas that enable interaction with key stakeholder groups.*

   The nature of a company's basic business model and the relationships it encourages between itself and its stakeholders will also influence how it can improve performance through corporate responsibility. It is important in this context to note that community-enabled innovation need not pertain solely to relationships with communities classically defined as those living around a manufacturing or retail site; community-enabled innovation pertains to what we call 'significant communities'. While business-to-business (B2B) models may have fewer points of interaction with retail consumers and the communities associated with retail outlets, they still have significant points of interaction with a wide range of other communities of interest, be they employees, business customers or suppliers. Thus, in footwear manufacture, improvements in factory labour conditions are dependent on the quality of relationships between factory suppliers and high street brand retailers. This is by no means a matter of 'B2B = No basis for community-enabled innovation' while 'B2C = Basis for community-enabled innovation'. There are strong examples (see the Dow case) of B2Bs providing private goods that do generate community-enabled innovation. What is critical in these cases is that the product and production process do not reduce points of interaction with communities, but rather provide the basis for engagement.

   Action implication: Advocates within companies should identify where the key points of interaction are with communities of interest that could provide insights into product, process, service or delivery. Where individual companies lack leverage, advocates may explore the basis of collective action as a way of reducing entry costs and increasing learning. Key areas such as ethical trade in supply chains have demonstrated that community-enabled innovation is not necessarily a zero-sum game and that innovation can be the result of collaborative action.

3. *The company can gain competitive advantage in its industry by differentiating itself through corporate responsibility.*

   Peer-to-peer competition within a single sector is another under-examined factor in determining how companies are likely to use engagement with communities to innovate and differentiate themselves from competitors. Thus, those campaigning in the United Kingdom for a fair return for agricultural producers in the South have engaged many high street food retailers, leading to the emergence of Sainsbury's and the Co-operative Wholesale Society as first movers and key players within the Ethical Trading Initiative (ETI), a cross-sector partnership established to take forward this agenda in the United Kingdom. While most of the other leading UK food retailers are also now involved, the leadership position of competitors does affect whether 'follower' companies engage with an issue in order themselves to innovate or engage in order to learn from other companies' innovation.

   Action implication: Advocates within companies need carefully to identify the trade-offs involved in differentiating themselves from competitors through community-enabled innovation. Key considerations include the relative lead competitors have, the entry costs and the relative corporate importance of the impact area (labour rights, energy use, etc).

4. *Strong cultures of learning or innovation within a company will significantly affect advocates' ability to generate community-enabled innovation.*
    Internal cultures of knowledge sharing and cross-unit functioning are indispensable if companies are to generate community-enabled innovation. A corporate responsibility team, or equivalent, housed in a silo separate from and deemed irrelevant to 'core' business functions is unlikely credibly to communicate any insights or patterns derived from engagement with civil society, suppliers, customers, regulators or other stakeholders.

    Poor group-wide tendencies to innovate will also make it harder for companies to make significant use of this team since the barriers to change will typically be deemed too high. As a positive counter-example, IBM's research labs have a good reputation for innovation and have reached across business units to draw on the networks of their community relations team to develop new software and hardware products for use by visually impaired groups.

    Action implication: Advocates within companies should identify formal and interpersonal ways of tapping into key knowledge management systems, whether these be through engaging with intranets or through engaging with key board members. Understanding the needs of key players in relation to group strategies is the key to channelling useful information derived from community-enabled innovations and leveraging up isolated cases into group-wide practices.

In summary, companies' own experience shows that community-enabled innovation can be an important approach for developing strategically important innovation. Such an approach to innovation isn't right for every company: a company's culture, competitive position and core skills help determine whether or not the company will be a supportive environment for this approach. Also, community-enabled innovation is not a guaranteed result from community engagement. But, as the cases summarized here show, properly managed community engagement can enable companies to capture and create strategically important benefits through community-enabled innovation.

John Sabapathy is a Senior Associate at AccountAbility.
www.accountability.org.uk

Companies and employees: working together to invest in communities

Graham Leigh, Charities Aid Foundation

Introduction

Companies are part and parcel of the United Kingdom's social fabric, creating the wealth that pays for the work of the public and voluntary sectors. But direct voluntary contributions to charities by companies, both in cash and in kind, have their place in making communities better places to live and work.

Charitable giving is the type of community investment that can be made free of tax. Charitable giving includes cash, employee time or materials and to benefit from this tax treatment the premise for these gifts is that they return negligible direct benefit to the company. Non-charitable community investment may seek clearer business gain. In either case it takes a clear strategic vision of what the company sets out to achieve to justify these programmes to company directors and shareholders.

Measuring and reporting contributions

Charitable contributions should be accounted for as a charge against income. This reduces profits and lowers the corporation tax liability accordingly. Measuring the value of all gifts may require a form of benchmarking, which looks at the relative outputs and impacts of giving. A standard benchmarking model such as that of the London Benchmarking Group may be helpful (www.lbg-online.net).

Managing budgets for donations

Any wholly charitable organization may receive a tax-effective charitable gift – it doesn't have to be registered with the Charity Commission. Many organizations, such as churches, are exempt from this requirement. Others may not have registered, as they fall below the Charity Commission's income threshold or they may be registered separately with HM Revenue and Customs for tax-efficient gifts. In any case, for an allowable tax concession on the gift it is important to validate the organization according to these criteria.

The Company Charity Account from the Charities Aid Foundation (CAF) includes an automatic validation facility for all outgoing payments. The account also allows charitable budgets to be kept separate from other business spend and rolled over from one financial year to the next (contact CAF Company Services on 020 7832 3000).

Where a large capital sum is intended to remain untouched and the interest is to be given away to charity, a corporate charitable trust might better fit the bill. For 'off-the-shelf' charitable trusts held in the company's name, contact CAF Trusts on 01732 520000. For further information on registering a company's own charitable trust, see the Charity Commission website at www.charity-commission.gov.uk.

New developments

Some forms of giving use various financial tools and tax-free incentives to create broader social benefit.

One alternative to making grants or donations is to bank a corporate fund for onward lending while retaining access after a given period of notice. (For further information, see www.charitybank.org.)

Loan finance offers the potential for charitable money to be recycled. Some charities carry out activity that doesn't fit ordinary financial models for risk and so they may find difficulty accessing loan finance, yet these organizations may be as capable of honouring a loan as ordinary businesses. At the same time they may also be capable of achieving impressive social returns on the money. Venture philanthropy is a model that brings together the best of giving and investing, and through intermediaries, such as Venturesome, money invested in social enterprise may be recycled several times. For further information, visit www.cafonline.org/venturesome.

Sponsorship and cause-related marketing

There are other legitimate corporate community investment (CCI) activities that may return a social benefit but are also aimed at business gain. Examples include corporate sponsorship of charities and cause-related marketing (CRM).

Sponsorships may benefit a company through public awareness of a company's brand or through a brand's positive association with a cause. If this association is clear and deliberate and provided as a condition of payment, then the benefit is tangible and should be charged to the sponsor, by the charity, at market rates. This is therefore a business activity for the charity and taxed accordingly. Typical sponsorship activities include prominent branding of advertisements or payment for a table at a charity banquet or a corporate box at a theatre.

Unlike sponsorship, CRM forms a positive association by using a charity's logo to help market a company product or service. BitC's Giving Now survey has discovered that 82 per cent of the population have been involved in a specific CRM programme (www.bitc.org.uk).

In a sponsorship or CRM agreement it is important for the charity and the company to guard against reputational risk, and for this reason it is prudent to use a commercial participation agreement with clearly stated objectives and expectations.

Government support for giving

According to the Home Office charitable giving strategy *A Generous Society*, published in November 2005, the government is committed to playing its part in meeting the challenge set out in the Giving Campaign launched in 2001, which was to double charitable donations in real terms within 10 years. One of the ways the government is doing this is by 'working with employers and employees so that existing schemes such as payroll giving and gifts of shares are maximised, and new approaches to social investment are fostered'. This has led to a number of initiatives being introduced, including the Payroll Giving Grants programme, designed to increase the number of small to medium-sized enterprises setting up and promoting payroll giving to their employees, and the Payroll Giving Quality Mark, which rewards employers for their commitment to workplace giving (www.payrollgivingcentre.org.uk).

CCI – how much is enough?

How much should a company contribute to social activity? There are some indicators, though ultimately it is the company's decision:

■ *Public opinion.* CCI, from charitable activity to sponsorship, CRM and employee involvement, can be seen as a balance of give and take. A good-practice programme is one that is considered by both the business and the community to give back as much as it takes out.

■ *Comparison with other companies.* As a broad indicator of 'how much', BitC set up the Per Cent Standard, whereby companies present their figures for total contributions in terms of cash, gifts in kind, management time and employee time as a proportion of pre-tax profits. Verified holders of the Per Cent Standard give in excess of 1 per cent. Of course, this target is easier for some companies to achieve than others, and this may depend not only on the value of the goods or services that a company supplies as well as its particular connection with social issues, but also on the way in which it is associated. For example, concern for shareholder reactions to unusually high levels of charitable contributions might make directors of public limited companies more cautious in the distribution of charitable gifts than those of privately owned companies.

■ *Meeting strategic objectives.* The ultimate measure of how much is enough is whether or not the company believes that it has met the strategic objectives that it set out to achieve and whether or not its opinion can be corroborated by the programme's stakeholders.

Money, in the right quantity and in the right place, can be the backbone of a credible, strategic and sustainable CCI programme. (For further information on the strategic argument for corporate philanthropy, see *The Competitive Advantage of Corporate Philanthropy* by Michael E Porter, http://www.isc.hbs.edu/firm-competitve.htm.)

Involving employees

Employee opinion is one of the main drivers for community involvement programmes. Employees consider the responsibilities of employers both to society and to the environment extremely important. The MORI survey *The Public's Views of Corporate Responsibility*, published in 2004, reported that 92 per cent of employees said that it was important that their own employer was responsible to society and the environment.

Involving employees in a company's community investment programme may demonstrate this commitment whilst giving a democratic element to the design of a programme. This may require a little company time and resource, but it can also reap great rewards in terms of staff motivation and morale, employee retention and skills sharing.

Volunteering

Employee volunteering schemes encourage employees to give their skills and either their personal time or a portion of the working day for the benefit of charitable organizations. The Home Office commissioned two citizenship surveys in 2001 and 2003 as part of the government's Active Community Agenda, which aims to create substantial progress towards a target of actively involving 1 million more people in their communities. The findings of the 2003 survey indicate that the proportion of the population in England over the age of 16 engaged in active community participation has risen from 48 per cent in 2001 to 51 per cent in 2003. The proportion involved in formal volunteering has not changed significantly; however, informal volunteering rose significantly from 34 per cent in 2001 (13.5 million people) to 37 per cent in

2003 (14.9 million people). Volunteering is clearly on the increase, and the Home Office, through its work with the Russell Commission, is encouraging this trend specifically with regard to increasing youth volunteering and civic service (http://www.russellcommission.org/).

Within the workplace, Volunteering England is one organization that can help to develop community programmes in line with strategic corporate and human resources objectives, as well as provide practical advice on matching companies to appropriate community groups. Employees in the Community Network (EitCN), an initiative set up by Volunteering England, provides companies with a regular forum for the exchange of knowledge and experience in this field. (For more information, visit http://www.volunteering.org.uk/workwith/ev.htm.)

Payroll giving

Payroll giving allows employees to give monthly donations to any UK charity direct from their pay. It's tax free, and a donation of, say, £10.00 would actually cost a basic-rate taxpayer just £7.80 in real terms, or a higher-rate taxpayer £6.00.

There are currently more than 578,000 payroll donors in the United Kingdom, and the latest figures from CAF show that £83 million was given through payroll giving in 2004/05, although payroll giving uptake is still small compared with the size of the potential market. The Home Office is specifically addressing this issue by investing in the Payroll Giving Grants programme for SMEs and the Payroll Giving Quality Mark (www.payrollgivingcentre.org.uk). Both are designed to encourage and reward employers that sign up to, and promote, payroll giving with cash and publicity incentives.

The facilitation and promotion of employee giving schemes can attract benefits similar to those of employee volunteering, eg improved staff morale, team building and satisfaction, as long as a scheme is introduced and promoted sensitively and with the involvement of staff. The administration for the payroll department is also minimal, and payroll giving agency charities provide the administration for collecting and splitting payments among hundreds of thousands of potential UK charity recipients.

The first thing to do in setting up a payroll giving scheme is to ensure that the company has a contract with an HM Revenue and Customs-approved agency charity. This contract is a legal requirement, and it ensures that funds are deducted from payroll and distributed within a reasonable time-frame. CAF is the largest of these organizations. (Contact details for all approved agencies are available at www.hmrc.gov.uk/payrollgiving/employers.)

There are professional organizations that can help to promote payroll giving. In most cases they will work on a commission basis, payable by the charity on a per-donor basis. This arrangement is effectively an outsourcing operation for fundraising, and many charities support this since it offers them reliable income for predictable costs. CAF's fundraising arm, Sharing the Caring, is the largest professional fundraising organization (www.sharingthecaring.org.uk). There are also examples of successful promotions where companies have promoted payroll giving using their own staff and resources.

Key principles for promoting involvement of employees in a community

Community involvement programmes are most successful when tailor-made to the needs of the individual company and its specific stakeholders. There are no generic rules or dos and don'ts for promoting the engagement of employees in these programmes, but there are some things that tend to help.

Laying the foundations

The type of response from employees can depend on the history and culture of community investment within the company, the benefits on offer and the appeal of the promotion; but often the success of a programme is dependent on planning. A well-planned programme will have greater appeal to employees than a gesture of charity and benevolence from out of the blue.

One way to clear the passage for successful engagement of employees in a CCI programme is to get their support ahead of a promotion. When offered the opportunity to give up their own time or money for the sake of the community, employees don't automatically accept that there is a link between their private interests and those of the business. They tend to like a little background information first, such as what the company is hoping to achieve – and why now?

Gathering information about what employees already do in the community and what support they would like can also help lay strong foundations for a promotion. Of course, the first thing that springs to mind is about managing expectations and setting boundaries on budget, timing, scope and policy, and openly stating these limitations at the launch stage of a programme. At the same time, the survey needs to offer genuine choice; there's little point in lobbying opinion if all the decisions have already been made.

A workforce that has been engaged in the design of a programme is more likely to take ownership of it and maintain sustained enthusiasm for the programme. This can result in genuine pride in its success, and create a positive impact on employee relations, morale and perceptions of the working environment.

Example benefits

Rockport UK is part of the Reebok corporation, and corporate social responsibility is at the top of its management agenda from labour standards right through to community involvement. Rockport wanted to match corporate values to practice and chose a project, in partnership with the Wildlife Trust, called Boots and Butterflies. Managing director Andy Loeber worked with colleagues to help clear Warton Crag, in Lancashire, of invading plant species. The work helped to increase the native food source of two endangered butterfly species, so it delivered great environmental benefits. The Wildlife Trust benefited from an extremely valuable volunteer resource, and there were plenty of business benefits besides.

Rockport already had a culture of 'work hard, play hard' and, once the management team had set the scene for the programme, employees quickly took ownership. Andy commented:

> This initiative was great for cross-functional relations. We didn't stick to our regular groups: people from Accounts worked with people from Marketing and so on. Boots and Butterflies really helped build team spirit... When we're all juggling different projects at different times, the biggest challenge is making time for it, but it has really been great fun and we now have lots of ideas for future events. It helped us understand the full potential for a great working environment, better productivity and a really strong team culture. The senior management team is behind it now more than ever.

Promotion tips

1. Companies often use matched giving programmes to bridge the gap between the company's direct contribution to the community and the contribution of its employees. Such programmes may have various constituent parts, eg matching proportions of employee donations to charity through payroll; matching one-off charitable gifts; matching employees' fund-raised money; matching employees' personal time with company time; or awarding gifts of cash for volunteering effort. These can be good options for making granting decisions in an inclusive, democratic and transparent way. They can also aid communication and measurement of the company's criteria for determining the success of a programme. (For assistance in planning, setting up and administering these programmes, call the CAF Company Services team on 020 7832 3000.)

2. Interaction is important. Programmes in which there is a good level of interaction between colleagues are not only likely to gain high levels of take-up, but also most likely to provide business benefits such as interdepartmental communication (throughout a company's hierarchy), skills sharing and team building. This is as true for payroll giving as for volunteering, where there needs to be a definite 'ask' from one colleague to another. Employees need to be given a clear and concise explanation of what they are being offered without being coerced into joining a scheme.

3. Pre-promotion information on the scheme can help build awareness ahead of time, which can encourage a warmer reception.

4. Partnering with charitable organizations or leveraging off existing campaigns such as National Giving Week (www.nationalgivingweek.org) can help provide a deeper insight into popular issues, and sometimes there is no substitute for their enthusiasm.

5. Standard literature can be provided by the agency charity or charity partner, or the company can produce its own information with their help.

6. Electronic promotion systems can help provide a convenient and immediate sign-up mechanism and therefore help build and maintain campaign momentum.
7. Whatever it is that the company decides to do, it should be fun. Employees remember a good time, even if it involves hard work.
8. Post-promotion information is a great way to maintain awareness of and enthusiasm for the programme for future years.

Corporate community investment is unlikely to be the answer for all of a company's responsibilities to society, but it can have an important place in a company's corporate responsibility strategy. A well-organized, inclusive and considered programme that is promoted effectively can have a generally positive impact on the company's operating environment and working environments, so, while many companies continue to struggle with the question of 'Why run a programme?', the resounding question for the enlightened might be 'Why not?'

Aiming for Waste Neutral

Dan Ryan, The Eden Project

Handling your waste better can improve your business. That's old news, isn't it? But often this statement is bandied about without providing the necessary information to make this vision a reality. Because a reality it surely can be.

Many businesses are rising to the challenge of effective waste management with varying degrees of success, and across all business sectors the challenges faced are diverse and tricky and require forethought, planning and the implementation of usable systems.

The Eden Project is a young business, being only five years old, and is presented with significant waste issues owing to the size and topography of the site and the scales and diversity of the business itself. Owing to the nature of these challenges, Eden has approached them in a dynamic way.

The blueprint for organizational behaviour adopted by Eden to take on one of the biggest challenges of modern sustainability is called Waste Neutral.

Setting the scene

Eden consists of many compartments adding up to a complex business venture owned by an educational charitable trust. Its core business is a large visitor destination in Cornwall attracting over 1 million people a year, providing the platform for the operation of local and global social enterprise projects split loosely into the fields of education, post-mining, conservation, commercial development and the arts.

A major element of this whole is the Waste Neutral Programme. Grounded in the on-site operational needs of the business, it also provides a research and development base for the trialling of new opportunities and technologies that can be communicated to the wider world. As a pilot programme under Eden's charitable wing, it has been largely funded through the Landfill Tax Credit Scheme.

A brief history

Devised in 2002 by Chris Hines, a founder of the widely acclaimed environmental pressure group Surfers against Sewage, the concept itself is simple. It builds on the traditional waste hierarchy of reduce, reuse and recycle but brings in a vital extra component – reinvest. This simply underlines the need to make better purchasing choices. Buy recycled, buy longer-lasting – buy better!

The Waste Neutral philosophy emphasizes the holistic nature of dealing with resources within any organization, integrating both waste minimization and purchasing practices. This signifies the need for ongoing commitment in reinvestment that ultimately aims to prevent the products sent for recycling merely becoming well-travelled landfill and provides a useful if slightly unwieldy measure of waste neutrality.

Eden's primary objective is to reduce the waste it creates. After this, it aims to reuse wherever possible, including literal reusages and more imaginative methods through the exhibit, landscaping and education teams. Following this, the aim is to recycle as much as is feasible of the remaining waste. Approximately 40 per cent of Eden's waste is organic, so at peak times all of this is destined for the composting systems. Other big recycling streams are glass, paper, card, plastics and metals and aggregates from our construction works. These are all collected through the traditional available means.

Using Eden as a case study, the Waste Neutral Programme is trialling new technologies in waste management, working closely with Eden's suppliers and the local business community, while also delivering significant educational work.

A crucial link in the Waste Neutral chain is Eden's purchasing policy. This defines what is bought and, therefore, what waste is created. If you can crack your purchasing, you can plan for the waste you have to deal with. This will, by its very nature, improve your efficiency and ultimately the overall sustainability of your business.

Waste Neutral is an unusual project for Eden, as it is at the same time both a stand-alone demonstration and research vehicle and an embedded element of Eden's way of being. A measure of success will be that all members of the Eden team will feel involved and as though they belong to Waste Neutral. This cross-company integration is essential for all businesses if they are to succeed in any sustainability or social enterprise.

It's not what we do, it's the way that we do it

The most important element of the technical operations of Waste Neutral was the construction in 2004 of the Waste Neutral Recycling Compound (WNRC). This complex has been purposely created in full view of all who enter the Eden estate with the main aim of bringing waste to the forefront of the public psyche. It is felt that this dislocation from the issue has been a stumbling block for too long and that the need to engage all sectors of society, including business, requires open acceptance of the implications, consequences and ultimately business success of effective waste management. By making waste a visual entity of the business and not hiding it from view, Eden hopes to overcome some of these barriers. We want people to become YIMBYs ('yes in my back yard').

The WNRC site itself contains storage areas for recyclates, skips for collection, the composter and a membrane bioreactor (MBR) filtration system. There is potential to expand and improve this development over time in response to future needs, including a weighbridge, sophisticated washing systems, green waste composting and so on. To facilitate the collection and movement of waste, Eden, local designers and bin experts Plastic Omnium have designed and developed the 'Eden Range' of recycling bins. These have appeared all around the site but they are designed for use in all public spaces. The range uses the new Wrap branding and offers some new features not found in conventional recycling systems. For instance, there is a clear front panel designed to take the correct materials for recycling to try to minimize the confusion faced by would-be recyclers. The bins are operated by foot pedal or by hand and are accessible by a wide user group. All these factors help improve the efficiency of the waste operation.

What can a business do really?

The three key elements of the Waste Neutral Programme, easily replicated by a range of business types, are the composter, supply chain work and construction initiatives.

Back to basics: the composter

The composter is a recent addition (summer 2005) to Eden's armoury in the battle against waste. Capable of consuming 500 kilograms of organic waste a day, or over 40 per cent of Eden's total daily waste, the Neter 30 composter was designed and built in Sweden by Susteco, where composting is an accepted community and business response to burgeoning waste problems. The composter is an aerobic in-vessel system and is primarily a research tool for Eden to identify whether it provides an effective solution for the disposal of organic waste, reducing the financial costs and environmental problems that result from landfilling it. The composter also has an important secondary purpose, which is reducing Eden's direct environmental, financial and social impacts on Cornwall's waste problem.

The UK has for too long not borne the full cost of sustainable waste management, and the financial burden of landfill costs is only going to increase with every passing year. Selecting a suitable system in the near future will place your business ahead of the game. The environmental impacts of landfills, such as greenhouse gas emissions and the leaching of harmful pollutants, are well understood. The benefits of environmental best practice such as this may not yet be in the forefront of your company's thinking, but in a changing world it may be foolish to underestimate them. These benefits could be very simple, such as the avoidance of fines and landfill charges, but may also present your business in a more favourable light to your competitors, customers and stakeholders.

The technology

Unlike larger co-composting facilities, the Neter is a small-scale community- or business-based in-vessel composting technology. The Neter seeks to divert bio-degradable waste from landfill, whilst reintroducing the proximity principle to waste management. All biological processes are carried out in the controlled environment of the cylinder, containing the odours and gases produced, to be dealt with by the associated bio-filter. The Neter works in conjunction with input/output material handling, shredding and in-built weighing equipment for inputs and outputs.

The Neter is a horizontal in-vessel composting system, working on a flow-through basis. The process of loading material into the front of the Neter, coupled with the rotating motion of the cylinder, moves the material through its length.

It should be noted that the Neter is a continuous rather than a batch composting facility. Thorough composting of the material within the process is ensured by the duration of stay and the rotating motion of the Neter. This unit is designed to have a minimum 40-day retention time, with the composting material passing through three distinct phases, producing fully composted, less biologically active, odour-free, safe compost.

Upon entering the composting chamber the material enters a thermophilic phase. This phase is characterized by high moisture content in the material and high temperatures created by the natural action of the process: typically 55–65 °C for 12–18 days. Pathogen kill-off is completed in this phase.

The material then moves into a mesophilic phase. Here there is reduction in moisture content and temperature. This stage is where most of the volume reduction occurs, and a temperature of 25–40 °C is maintained for a typical retention time of 18–24 days.

Following this is a final maturation phase of composting, lasting approximately 10–15 days. Here moisture levels are reduced further, and a temperature of approx-imately 20 °C is maintained.

The temperatures achieved are dependent on several factors, including the nature of the food waste, moisture levels and aeration of the material. Temperature is monitored at five locations throughout the cylinder and logged constantly. This information is used to provide evidence that the waste has been treated to the required standard and provides an understanding of how the differing phases work simultaneously within one vessel.

All air extracted from the Neter is treated via the integral bio-filter, which uses a natural process to eliminate odours. While the bio-filter has not been tested on this scale before, initial tests have proved successful and in similar applications there has been an odour reduction of up to 98 per cent.

This system differs from most in its long retention time, and Eden and Susteco believe the technology can fully comply with the pathogen removal levels required and be capable of meeting prescribed standards of treatment. The team will also undertake a programme of testing to ensure that the composted output meets standards approved by Defra for the treatment of catering waste via in-vessel composting.

However, the Neter is the first aerobic in-vessel facility of its size in the UK and one of the first in Europe. As such, the initial investment was relatively large (approaching £200,000) but, with the savings in current and predicted transport and landfill costs, the investment is expected to pay for itself within 10 years.

Getting into your supply chain

A considerable amount of time was spent at the outset researching sources of available information on Eden's incoming and outgoing resources, and in trialling ways of getting the data needed from both external suppliers and internal teams.

During 2005 a regular Waste Neutral Purchasing Forum was set up. This group looks at how Eden purchases items, reducing resource buy-in, resource reuse on-site, increasing the purchasing of items with recycled material content and ensuring that items can be recycled at the end of their life. The first fruits of this work are indicated by greatly reduced packaging waste emanating from the catering units.

Eden tries to reuse as much packaging as possible, but when this is not possible tries to ensure it is recycled. Assessing the use of compostable packaging, most notably in sandwich wrapping that could go through the food composter, is now ongoing. If successful this would not only reduce the waste being sent to landfill, but also result in extra compost to feed the plants – further reducing the need for bought-in material.

One of the initial parts of the supply chain project has been to pull together existing pieces of information, review them and assess what information is still needed, if any, and how it can be obtained.

At this point Waste Neutral had been measured mainly by a black box approach, with figures for reinvestment through retail, plus exit figures from the Waste Neutral Compound going to disposal or recycling. These figures appear in a 'Big facts and figures' document along with other relevant statistics. 'Big facts and figures' is an overall document for assessing overall resource use, not necessarily Waste Neutral behaviour. There are figures that are of use but most of the items arriving on-site are not considered (in weight terms) and it is this area (measuring what comes on to site) where most pitfalls arise.

A consultant put together a report entitled 'Waste Neutral at Eden – measured progress'. This document is a snapshot of ideas on how the Waste Neutral concept can progress, showing in particular the different waste/resource flow 'channels' and the development of the datasheet process whereby all suppliers are asked to fill in details of the weights and materials of the products they supply to Eden and any thoughts they have on how the product or the associated packaging could be improved from a waste standpoint. The conclusion was that, although a useful tool, the datasheets were not the most effective way of assessing waste neutrality. They require much commitment from internal departments and consistent data to be returned from suppliers, leaving much to their subjective viewpoint and commitment to the concept. Practically it has been more successful to identify the top suppliers and products using a Pareto analysis approach that meant going for big-impact hits. These have included a switch from disposable to washable cutlery and crockery in the restaurants and more recycled paper usage.

The recycling figures from the WNRC give 'exit' figures from the project and are very useful. Ideally these now correlate with the 'input' figures. Recent progress has identified waste neutrality for individual resource floors ie wood, plastics and metals.

Problems and pitfalls

The biggest challenge with assessing waste neutrality is the lack of a central purchasing system. At Eden there is no purchasing department, and purchasing decisions are made by many people from the full range of departments. This is coupled with the fact that, with the exception of catering and retail, there is currently no way of establishing historically what stock has been bought in. If a decision were made to have a centralized purchasing unit, this would make Waste Neutral easier to implement.

Cutting construction waste

Eden is world renowned for its inspirational buildings and landscaping, and it is natural that this sector is an important part of the Waste Neutral Programme. Working with Eden's sustainable construction adviser, Eden's build partnership, led by the McAlpine Joint Venture, has adopted the concept. This has involved the separation of waste for recycling as well as significant waste reduction through design and building practices, the use of recyclates and recyclable material in the build, site waste management plans, and the training of subcontractors. This work has already been recognized in a number of national award categories, and the benefits to a business of cutting waste in small- or large-scale construction projects become immediately obvious. Buying less material saves money, and getting rid of less waste material is equally productive.

Summary

■ Actively measure resource 'inputs' and 'exits' and reflect the findings in your actions.
■ Place a firm emphasis on purchasing policy to streamline your operations and make waste less of a burden on your company and the environment.
■ Where possible, deal with your own waste in sustainable ways.
■ Long-term thinking and investment now may reap rewards in the very near future.

Let's talk rubbish

Tim Price, Severnside Recycling

The message bearing down on the UK's business community is clear – each organization must take responsibility for reducing the impact of its business on our environment. What's more, just about every element of our society demands it. Whether it's local government, national government, suppliers or ultimately our customers and the wider society in general, the message is the same – reduce, reuse, recover, recycle more and landfill less.

Organizations must respond to this message and not for any one reason in particular. There are two main issues associated with dealing with waste arisings. The first is cost and the second is legislation. There is no waste stream produced that is not covered by legislation of some nature. In fact currently, legislation such as the Packaging Directive, WEEE Directive, Landfill Directive, Animal By-Products Regulations and Hazardous Waste Regulations all place duties on organizations to treat waste in a responsible manner. It is possible to 'buy' compliance with legislation but this, in a competitive economy with decreasing cost bases seen as a priority, is not a tenable solution. Conversely non-compliance with organizations' social, environmental and ethical responsibilities is not a viable alternative.

The alternative is to develop an approach that understands the reasons why waste arises in an organization and, after minimizing its production, to employ effective methods of recovery to ensure disposal is minimized. There is no disputing that commitment is required, but when research is pointing to the fact that a company's waste costs can be up to 2 per cent of turnover, let alone profit, the effort may be justified.

get us in...

...and we'll talk
complete rubbish

Because at Severnside that's what we do. Only by discussing your waste streams in the context of your business can we deliver you cost effective recycling & waste management systems. More than that, we're ready to start talking about your rubbish as a resource, a resource with a value – now who's talking rubbish?

Severnside Facilities Management Centre: 0800 7 831 831

email: complete.services@severnside.com

www.severnside.com

SEVERNSIDE
You, Us and The Environment

Maximum diversion from landfill at the most economic cost, along with reducing the risk of environmental non-compliance, can be expensive in terms of knowledge and human resources. This is why understanding the patterns and practices of waste management within organizations is an essential part of delivering the cost benefits of sustainable waste management. Benchmarking is an essential tool in establishing best practices, enabling us to learn from 'best in class' examples. As such, it is vital in helping organizations to evaluate current practices. The important next stage is to digest and share this information, to help us all understand what is needed to push forward towards truly sustainable waste management practices.

If organizations view waste not as a redundant property but rather as a valuable scare resource, then the economic benefits of sustainable waste management can be delivered. A holistic approach to waste management, with sustainability written into it, will allow businesses to become more efficient and, yes, more profitable. This is achieved not only by curbing spiralling waste disposal costs, but also by generating revenue back into the business.

Developing a strategy – the Environmental Value Chain

So far we have discussed how the impact on businesses of their use of natural resources and their production of waste is no longer a peripheral issue. Moreover, these issues are now core to the competitiveness of an organization. Rapidly rising energy costs have seen high energy users close production at peak prices, and waste disposal and environmental compliance costs appear to be forever soaring skywards. Nowhere else (except perhaps with pension provisions) are organizations faced by cost lines that are increasing so harshly, with no apparent opportunity to mitigate these cost escalations.

Two factors seek to exacerbate these problems: the compound effect of continuing legislative intervention by both the UK and the EU parliament, and a lack of clarity within organizations as to the true accountability for decisions that affect environmental matters and costs.

However, it is possible to develop a methodology to map, track and clarify the lines between environmental costs and the traditional core value chain of an organization. The model is called the 'Environmental Value Chain'.

By mapping the decisions that impact on environmental performance and resource usage, it is possible to map the value of these decisions. The value is expressed in terms of both positive and negative contributions to the business. For example, a type of transit packaging may be chosen because it is cheaper to procure, but the packaging may have high compliance and disposal costs. When all the value (purchase price benefit less compliance and disposal costs) is understood, the organization may have a new view of the true impact of that decision.

The Environmental Value Chain can provide a framework to enable the holistic or total value to be established for the entire business. The process follows simple input and output principles, with the exercise following the procurement of services and resources through manufacturing, warehousing and distribution to eventual sale.

In summary, organizations cannot maximize their returns without having a focused environmental strategy that delivers lowest-cost compliance and opportunities to exploit the company's position. Recycling and waste management issues need to be placed at the very forefront of business planning. The Environmental Value Chain adopts the principles of the National Waste Hierarchy to achieve this. Ultimately, by following these principles and exploring sustainable alternatives to disposal through landfill, organizations can at last begin to move towards a goal of zero waste.

The construction industry: responding to the rise of sustainability and corporate social responsibility

Peter Bonfield, BRE Construction

With an annual output of some £75 billion, the construction industry plays a major role in the UK economy, accounting for around 8 per cent of GDP and directly employing 1.5 million people (1 in 14 of the total working population). There are an estimated 164,000 construction companies in the United Kingdom, the vast majority of these being small and medium-sized enterprises (SMEs) with fewer than 24 workers.

The sector has profound and extensive environmental, economic and social impacts, and is therefore a key player in delivering government policy objectives on climate change, energy, resource use, waste minimization, housing, transport, urban regeneration and sustainable communities. Waste from construction and demolition materials, including soil, equals 70 million tonnes annually (29 per cent of UK controlled waste), with an estimated 13 million tonnes of this made up of materials delivered to building sites but never used. Annually, the industry produces three times the waste generated by all UK households combined, and the amount of construction materials used each year is equivalent to 6 tonnes per head of the UK population. About 17 per cent of waste going to landfill sites is directly related to construction, with indirect arisings such as quarrying and other waste doubling this figure. Around 50 per cent of UK CO_2 emissions are from energy used for heating, cooling, ventilation and lighting in buildings. The sector accounts for 60 per cent of all timber used in the United Kingdom, the majority of it imported.

Clearly, moves to minimize waste, reduce pollution and improve resource use within the sector would make a significant contribution to national sustainable development objectives as well as boosting the sector's profitability and improving its reputation as a socially and environmentally responsible employer. This chapter looks at some of the initiatives that are driving forward improvements across the industry.

Rethinking construction

In July 1998 the influential report *Rethinking Construction* was published by the Construction Task Force, chaired by Sir John Egan. The report aimed to provide a blueprint for the future long-term competitiveness and performance of the construction industry in the United Kingdom by improving efficiency, minimizing waste and focusing on quality. The improvement targets identified in the report were to:

■ reduce capital cost by 10 per cent per year;
■ reduce construction time by 10 per cent per year;
■ reduce defects by 20 per cent per year;
■ reduce accidents by 20 per cent per year;
■ increase predictability by 20 per cent per year;
■ increase productivity by 10 per cent per year;
■ increase turnover and profits by 10 per cent per year.

Following this, the Construction Best Practice Programme (CBPP) and the Movement for Innovation (M4I) were set up to take forward the report's recommendations. CBPP set up a comprehensive website and a network of best-practice clubs, and developed other innovative resources and tools. It worked with industry groups to develop key performance indicators (KPIs). M4I concentrated on promoting demonstration projects that demonstrated the 'Rethinking construction' principles. The programme comprised 374 demonstration projects with a combined value of almost £7 billion covering the whole industry, including housing and local government clients and all types of construction work: new-build, refurbishment, repairs and maintenance. KPIs were used to monitor progress. These revealed that the 'Rethinking construction' projects outperformed the industry average in all areas, with the highest scores being for safety and reduced environmental impact. The demonstration projects achieved astonishing savings: client construction costs 6 per cent below the industry average, accident rates 61 per cent lower and profitability 2 per cent higher. If these figures are extrapolated to apply to a third of the UK construction industry, the cost of accidents could be reduced by £1.2 billion annually, client construction costs could decrease by £1.4 billion and industry profits could increase by £446 million.

Operating in a complex environment

The construction industry is used to operating in a heavily regulated business environment. It is subject to a large number of governmental and legislative requirements that in themselves drive forward sustainability: the planning system, environmental impact assessment, the contaminated land regime, the Climate Change Levy, landfill tax, aggregates tax, the Building Regulations, etc. There will be further legislation on water, energy and planning, and from January 2006 the industry will need to meet the requirements of the EU Energy Performance of Buildings Directive (EPBD), which requires that all buildings have an energy label whenever they change ownership or tenancy.

Following the Better Buildings Summit held in October 2003, John Prescott, Margaret Beckett and Patricia Hewitt established the Sustainable Building Task Group (SBTG) to identify how government and industry could improve the quality and sustainability of new and refurbished buildings. One of the key recommendations coming out of the group's report, published in May 2004, was the establishment of a Code for Sustainable Buildings, based on the Building Research Establishment's Environmental Assessment Method (BREEAM) and EcoHomes. The Code would be used by planning authorities to set standards higher than the Building Regulations for energy, water and waste. 'When you get local authorities, the government and planning authorities making a label or code higher than the Building Regulations, then the industry will respond,' says David Strong, Managing Director of BRE Environment.

There are numerous non-statutory pressures too, notably on corporate social responsibility (CSR) reporting: the rise of the socially responsible investor, greater community activism, shifting client expectations and growing pressure to comply with corporate good governance rules.

Attracting and retaining high-calibre staff is a well-documented and perennial problem. The construction industry's relatively poor reputation and the perceived lack of job security contribute to its difficulty in employing well-qualified staff. The Construction Industry Training Board estimated an annual shortfall of 6,500 tradespeople in the building trades by 2005. These and other issues are fuelling interest in innovative construction techniques and new construction technologies, including prefabrication and off-site manufacturing.

Lean construction

Borrowing from the concept of lean manufacturing, lean construction is about the management of construction processes to deliver more value to the customer, with the elimination of waste being a core feature. Lean construction focuses on maximizing customer value by seeking to remove all non-value-adding components and processes while improving those that add value.

The Construction Lean Improvement Programme (CLIP), managed by the Building Research Establishment (BRE) in partnership with Constructing Excellence and supported by the Department of Trade and Industry, has adapted lean tools and techniques to remove waste from all levels of the construction process, including materials and energy use. CLIP engineers provide practical intervention, coaching and team development services for UK construction firms that are seeking to improve their business, management, construction and supplier management processes. Productivity is increased by diagnosing current practices and processes, challenging them, and implementing improvements with the customer's team.

Following a successful pilot scheme in 2002 in which certain projects saw a 40 per cent improvement in productivity and profitability, a five-year programme was launched in 2003, with more than 60 companies initially expressing interest. Project director Martin Watson believes that CLIP could be of great benefit to many construction companies by encouraging them to look at what they do in a fresh way: 'CLIP is set to have a significant impact on the long-term sustainability of the industry. If the results from the pilot are replicated across the rest of the industry, then widespread performance improvement is imminent. Companies can expect to make improvements of at least 20 per cent to quality, cost and/or delivery.'

BRE offers services for both manufacturers and contractors on modern methods of construction, such as off-site manufacture, timber and light-gauge steel frame, prefabrication, and tunnelform concrete casting. For manufacturers, it provides advice on product design and development, and can test and certify the performance of new products and construction methods to ensure conformity to Building Regulations and other relevant standards. For main contractors, design management and supply chain management advice is available to help them fulfil a sustainable brief. To help companies manage their waste more efficiently, BRE has developed a benchmarking tool, SMARTWaste, which enables construction firms to measure the source, type, quantity, cause and cost of their waste.

Client demand

Increasing client demand for more sustainable buildings is a key issue for the construction sector. Companies such as Sainsbury's, Shell, BP and BT have adopted high-profile CSR policies that require their premises to be 'clean and green', with high energy efficiencies and recycled material content, access to public transport, natural ventilation, and low emissions. The design and construction process needs to be to the highest standard, generating low amounts of waste, noise and nuisance, using water and energy efficiently, and specifying recycled or sustainable materials, such as Forest Stewardship Council-certified timber, where appropriate.

Increasingly, clients are turning to tools such as BREEAM for assessing and improving the environmental performance of offices, schools, supermarkets and industrial units. A parallel scheme for housing, called EcoHomes, is also available.

The government, which is responsible for 40 per cent of total UK construction industry output, has set itself the target of achieving a BREEAM 'Excellent' rating for all new public buildings; this is acting as a key driver to shift the sector towards more sustainable outcomes and ways of working. English Partnerships now requires BREEAM 'Excellent' for its developments, while the Housing Corporation makes EcoHomes 'Excellent' a provision of funding for housing associations.

Designing environmentally friendly buildings is extremely complex, so BRE has developed a software program, ENVEST, to help designers identify those aspects that have the greatest influence on a building's environmental impact. And in order to ensure the credibility of 'green' building materials and products, BRE's Certified Environmental Profiling scheme offers a universal measuring system to help designers and specifiers identify suitable materials while enabling manufacturers to demonstrate the environmental credentials of their products.

A collaborative approach reaps dividends

The construction sector is characterized, perhaps more than any other, by its fragmentation into hundreds of thousands of small companies, many of them sole traders. Getting the CSR message across in these circumstances is exceptionally difficult. A report by the Sustainable Construction Task Group, published in December 2003, concluded that most construction industry companies remain ignorant of the benefits that sustainable practices can bring.

Consequently, leading construction companies and industry bodies have focused on partnerships and integration to ensure that everyone in the construction process and supply chain can engage with the CSR agenda, from the smallest operator to the biggest. The Strategic Forum for Construction has set a target for 20 per cent of construction projects to be undertaken by integrated teams and supply chains by the end of 2004, and 50 per cent by the end of 2007. To this end, it is piloting an Integration Toolkit, which is now being used on demonstration projects. The toolkit promises faster delivery times, improved profitability, reduced accidents and greater customer satisfaction.

In order to improve competitiveness, rise to environmental and social challenges and provide better value for its customers, the construction sector has developed an impressive range of demonstration projects, best-practice initiatives, management toolkits, supply chain networks and innovative working practices, and these are starting to reap tangible benefits. The sector's collaborative approach offers valuable lessons to other manufacturing industries.

External relationships: legal overview

James Samuel, Simmons & Simmons

External relationships are not primarily a legal issue, although there is a legal obligation to consult or inform external stakeholders in a number of situations relevant to sustainability. For example, as part of an application for planning permission, or making information available to the public, companies whose processes are regulated under Integrated Pollution Control are required by law to report emissions to air and water of certain pollutants above a specific threshold to the Environment Agency.

The opportunity for shareholder views on matters such as investments to be made known at annual general meetings (which are a legal requirement) is increasingly being utilized by shareholders. To assist shareholders, regulations came into force in March 2005 that made it mandatory for directors of a listed company to prepare an annual Operating and Financial Review (OFR). This requires companies to report on their environmental and social impact. The Chancellor of the Exchequer announced in November 2005 that the OFR would be abolished, as the requirement went beyond the requirements of the EU Accounts Modernization Directives. However, following the commencement of judicial review proceedings by Friends of the Earth into this decision, the Chancellor reversed his position, but announced a consultation on the future of the OFR. Nevertheless, organizations often adopt voluntary engagement on sustainability issues, in particular where there is a clearly identifiable issue associated with an industry.

The United Nations Economic Commission for Europe (UNECE) Aarhus Convention is a new kind of international environmental agreement. The convention is premised on the concept that sustainable development can only be achieved through the involvement of all stakeholders. The convention has three 'pillars': access to information, public participation and access to justice. Around 40 countries, including the UK, have signed up to it, as has the European Union. In general the goalposts have moved significantly in favour of disclosure of information since the Freedom of Information Act 2000 and Environmental Information Regulations 2004 came into force. Both pieces of legislation give certain rights to access information held by public authorities and encourage public authorities proactively to make information available to the general public.

Increasingly, individuals and companies are requiring their suppliers to have adopted a formal environmental management system, for example ISO 14001 or the European Eco-Management and Audit Scheme (EMAS), as one of their formal contractual requirements. Imposing sustainability requirements on suppliers is an important issue, and environmental improvements can be delivered in this way, often in advance of formal legal requirements. A good example of this is the EC Directive on Waste Electrical and Electronic Equipment, where automotive manufacturers required supplier compliance with its requirements well in advance of its formal implementation dates.

5

Energy, land use and the environment

Energy use: legal overview

Jacqui O'Keeffe, Simmons & Simmons

There has been a great deal of new legislation in the field of energy and the environment, particularly in relation to energy use, greenhouse gas emissions and renewable energy sources. As well as energy-specific regulation, the environmental impacts of energy production are also taken into account within other regulatory regimes. For example, Pollution Prevention and Control (PPC) requires that the best available techniques are used in connection with emissions and operations for many energy production and combustion processes, and requires energy efficiency measures for other energy-intensive installations.

Many of the drivers for change in the approach to energy issues come from Europe. For example, the Renewables Directive (2001/77/EC), which was adopted in September 2001, requires each EU member state to commit to specific targets for renewable energy. The recitals to the directive state that the Community recognizes the need to promote renewable energy sources as a priority measure, given that their exploitation contributes to environmental protection and sustainable development. The directive required member states to adopt national indicative targets for future consumption of electricity from renewable sources, compatible with their Kyoto targets. Member states were also required to provide an outline of the measures taken, or planned, to achieve this. This includes putting in place a system of guarantees regarding the origin of electricity produced from renewable energy sources, supervised by a competent body.

In the UK a 'Renewables Obligation' (RO) was imposed on licensed electricity suppliers from April 2002, creating a unified GB-wide system of tradable green certificates known as ROCs. The intention of the RO is to provide a stable market that will in turn encourage investment in new renewable electricity-generating capacity, helping the UK achieve its 10 per cent renewable energy target by 2010, and further targets are set thereafter until 2027.

The EU Emissions Trading Scheme (EU ETS) began in January 2005, and is a cap-and-trade scheme to reduce carbon emissions. Companies with high-emission plants are set annual emissions reduction targets, to be met either by lowering emissions or by buying 'allowances' from other companies. The second phase of the scheme is due to begin in 2008, and new targets for this phase are currently under review.

Emissions reductions are also effected in 'Annex I' countries (those that have taken on emission reduction or limitation targets under the Kyoto Protocol) by Joint Implementation (JI) and in non-Annex I countries by the Clean Development Mechanism (CDM). The JI mechanism operates on the basis of emission reductions that arise from project investments in other countries with their own Kyoto emission targets, with CDM the equivalent in developing countries that don't have their own Kyoto emission targets (non-Annex I countries). Credits are given for funding projects that reduce greenhouse gas emissions – Emission Reduction Units (ERUs) under the JI (from 2008) and Certified Emission Reduction Credits (CERs) under the CDM. The 2004 European 'Linking Directive' may allow companies participating in the EU ETS to use carbon credits from JI and CDM projects for compliance, despite the fact that there is at present no international scheme fully in place to regulate the Kyoto mechanisms. Individual member states must decide whether to allow or place a limit on the number of credits that can be used by companies in their countries that participate in the scheme. The ERUs credits have been excluded from the first phase of the EU ETS, but may be included from the second-phase review.

Directive 2002/91/EC on the energy performance of buildings is being implemented by the government through amendments to the Building Regulations. The government is also proposing to publish a new Code for Sustainable Homes to set star ratings for the energy efficiency of new homes. The objective of these measures is to improve the energy performance of buildings within the Community, with member states required to set minimum energy performance requirements for all buildings, subject to specified exemptions. When buildings are constructed, sold and rented out, an energy performance certificate must be made available allowing consumers to compare the energy performance of different buildings.

The DTI has just published an Energy Review entitled 'The Energy Challenge', addressing all aspects of the energy system, including both energy supply and energy demand, and setting out proposals to secure clean, affordable energy for the long term. Concerns over energy security and increased dependence on imported energy and impact on climate change have, for example, led to the government looking again at the use of nuclear power to meet some of the country's energy needs, as most existing nuclear power stations are scheduled to close over the coming 20 years. New technologies are also being examined, such as carbon capture and storage (CCS), to reduce the amount of carbon emitted into the atmosphere. The process captures carbon emitted during the generation process and stores it in geological formations (eg depleted gas fields or deep saline aquifers). In June 2005 the government announced a Carbon Abatement Technology (CAT) Strategy committing money and time to developing such technologies, meaning that there are likely to be further developments in this area in the coming years.

Another important element in the UK government's energy policy, as set out in the Energy White Paper, is cogeneration, or combined heat and power (CHP). CHP is a fuel-efficient energy technology that, unlike conventional forms of power generation, puts to use the by-product heat that is normally wasted to the environment. CHP can increase the overall efficiency of fuel use to more than 75 per cent (compared with around 40 per cent from conventional electricity generation). Furthermore, because it often supplies electricity locally, CHP can also avoid transmission and distribution losses. The government is using grants, fiscal incentives and regulatory support to encourage CHP.

Energy efficiency

Tim Ashmore, TAES Energy

Meeting the energy challenges ahead

The combined effect of higher energy prices and the target for reducing CO_2 emissions by 2010 has been that UK industry is coming under increasing pressure to improve the environmental performance and cost-effectiveness of its processes and buildings. However, unpredictable consumption patterns and the apparent difficulties of devising energy efficiency programmes for commercial sites dissuade many firms from trying to implement energy-saving measures.

The low price of energy in past years did little to encourage energy efficiency initiatives, especially as cost savings could be more easily made by reducing the unit cost of electricity. However, it is clear that a huge amount of energy is now being wasted through a lack of action on the part of energy users. The government-funded Carbon Trust estimates that every year £12 billion of energy is wasted across the United Kingdom. This represents a staggering 30 per cent of the country's consumption, with UK businesses losing up to £400 million per year just by neglecting to implement energy efficiency measures. In the past two years or so, energy costs have risen significantly and, if they continue to rise over the next few years, the current level of energy wastage will cost UK industry more and more. Of course, this rise in the base rate also means that the payback period for efficiency measures already taken will begin to shorten, thereby rewarding organizations that are addressing energy conservation.

Public pressure

With soaring oil prices and a renewed debate over climate change and security of supply, energy has been high on the news agenda. Public concern over energy efficiency and global warming is increasing. There is also a growing demand for 'corporate greenness' that seems unrelenting, and companies are faced with an increased public awareness of corporate social responsibility. Reducing energy consumption offers a fast and politically acceptable alternative to traditional areas of cost cutting. And these savings are sustainable. But it's not just about cost control. Reducing energy consumption offers relief from these growing environmental pressures on business.

UK government and EU action

In addition to the financial burden arising from the increase in energy costs, industrial users may also find themselves liable for penalties imposed by the government on wasteful users. In February 2003 the government published the Energy White Paper, confirming its views regarding Britain in a low-carbon future. The paper strongly stated the need for more renewable energy and greater energy efficiency, and outlined demanding goals for reductions in CO_2 emissions, with targets or 'ambitions' set for 2010, 2020 and 2050. The government aims to cut the level of carbon emitted over the next 50 years by 60 per cent.

In April 2004 the Environment Secretary, Margaret Beckett, unveiled the government's implementation plan, which outlined how it will deliver the strategy set out in the Energy White Paper. *Energy Efficiency: The government's plan for action* sets out how the government aims to tackle climate change, cutting carbon emissions by an extra 12 million tonnes through energy efficiency within the next six years, and saving more than £3 billion a year on energy costs. The strategy includes a range of measures, such as changes to the Building Regulations, to raise energy efficiency standards, doubling the level of Energy Efficiency Commitment activity from 2005 to 2011, and new energy service pilot schemes through which energy suppliers can offer energy-efficient packages to customers.

The EU Emissions Trading Scheme (EU ETS) came into force in 2005. This is a European-wide initiative to incentivize larger businesses to reduce carbon emissions. The first phase runs from 2005 until the end of 2007, and early indications show that there may have been an over-allocation of carbon allowances. The likelihood, as a consequence, is that Phase 2 allocations, starting in 2008, will be much tighter. UK businesses should therefore start to prepare for this now.

Renewable energy

Actions aimed at limiting carbon emissions are already under way in the form of the Climate Change Levy (CCL), the EU ETS and the Renewables Obligation, which requires electricity suppliers to sell a defined, and annually increasing, percentage of renewable electricity. The EU Directive on Fuel Labelling, which came into effect at the end of July 2004, gave suppliers one year in which to comply with new regulations. Suppliers are obliged to state clearly where their energy is sourced and the percentages from each source. The government wants to see 10 per cent of the country's electricity power derived from renewable sources by 2010 and 20 per cent by 2020.

As renewable energy sources are currently relatively scarce yet high in demand, renewable energy commands a premium. Organizations looking to improve their environmental performance with renewable energy should plan ahead and communicate their needs to their energy supplier sooner rather than later to secure the volume they require.

While the cost of renewable energy is expected to fall as supply increases, the government itself estimates that the various measures proposed in its White Paper will add between 10 and 25 per cent to industrial electricity prices. This implies that, if UK firms are to avoid a large financial burden, they need to act soon to get energy efficiency measures in place.

Measuring and monitoring energy wastage

As these measures continue to take effect, UK industry is realizing that there is a growing cost implication for firms neglecting properly to address their energy wastage.

The key to avoiding unnecessary cost is to know how much energy is used and where, so that wastage can be identified and eliminated. Of course, those organizations already involved with CCL exemption agreements are familiar with the need to monitor and record their energy consumption, to be sure of meeting their targets. Measurement can itself be seen as a cost, but, given that it can help firms fulfil their CCL obligations and also address energy wastage across the whole organization, use of such a measurement system is extremely beneficial.

There are a number of specialized products to help businesses monitor energy consumption and costs. Some of these are available from energy brokers and suppliers directly as part of their 'added value' services. However, more bespoke services and products can be provided from energy management and software companies. In each case consumptions can be monitored against variables that affect usage, trends and benchmarking against other sites and performance indices.

Implementing energy efficiency

Energy efficiency measures often fall at the first hurdle, owing to the perceived high cost of implementing and maintaining such initiatives. Many organizations tend to view energy as an uncontrollable overhead, but this is far from true. There are several simple measures firms can take to cut energy wastage, many of which are free.

Of course, the cheapest unit of energy is the unit not used, and staff awareness of simple energy-saving measures can save an organization a considerable amount of money. Even a small business can substantially cut its energy costs by merely turning off computers, monitors, photocopiers and televisions overnight, rather than leaving them on standby. Imagine the energy wasted, and hence the cost generated, by a large organization leaving all its computers and monitors on standby over the Christmas holiday. Lighting often accounts for around half of all energy used, so turning off lights, especially high-powered task lighting, is a very effective form of energy efficiency.

The Carbon Trust and some energy suppliers offer free posters showing ways to use less energy, thereby raising awareness of the importance of energy-saving measures 'on the shop floor'. Recent research carried out by London Energy has revealed that it may be possible to persuade staff to apply simple energy-saving measures. The survey found that almost 80 per cent of companies believed that staff are responsive to simple energy-efficient policies such as turning off computers and photocopiers overnight, given suitable encouragement.

The second stage of improving energy efficiency is to ensure that energy-using equipment is maintained correctly and regularly. This applies also to control systems for heating, air-conditioning, etc. Poorly maintained plant and controls will almost always use more energy than necessary, and often the cost of maintenance can be more than balanced by the savings from the consequent reduction in energy consumption.

While these simple measures are a very good starting point, other routes to energy efficiency, and hence cost savings, do require some initial investment. In terms of premises, buildings should be well insulated and have draught-proof doors and windows. Heating and air-conditioning units should be regularly serviced and well maintained. As 25 per cent of the United Kingdom's carbon dioxide emissions come from lost heat emitted from buildings, improved energy efficiency is a primary element of the UK Climate Change Programme set out by the Office of the Deputy Prime Minister. Saving heat reduces energy bills and lowers harmful emissions. Recent amendments to Building Regulations together with the forthcoming EU Directive on Energy in Buildings will oblige companies to maintain energy-efficient buildings.

Companies that have energy-intensive core processes need to undertake a cost–benefit analysis to ensure that old or poorly maintained equipment is not costing them more in the long term than the upfront cost of upgrading to more energy-efficient machinery now. The efficiency of high-energy-use machinery is absolutely vital when tackling energy wastage. While these measures may require a large initial outlay, the consequent savings in energy usage are immediate and ongoing, especially when the rising cost of energy is factored into the equation. Of course, these measures also have knock-on benefits for the environment.

Alternative financing

Many businesses may not feel able to invest directly in energy-saving initiatives that require high upfront capital. There are alternative funding arrangements.

The Carbon Trust provides a number of schemes to assist in resourcing energy efficiency measures. These include free initial energy audits, enhanced capital allowances (tax breaks) for certain energy-saving equipment, and interest-free loans for investment in new plant.

WIND DIRECT: A CASE STUDY IN COST SAVINGS THROUGH RENEWABLE ENERGY

Thomas S. Murley
Director, Energy Investments, HgCapital, London

Introduction

Among the many misconceptions about renewable energy is that it is always more expensive than conventional energy, and that companies that use renewable energy to are sacrificing bottom line profits. In many cases this is true, although with rising oil and gas costs and pollution costs (in the form of carbon emissions costs) now a factor, many renewable technologies can compete with conventional technologies. However, in many industrial applications renewable power creates cost savings. For example, in Scandinavia, heat and power for paper mills and sawmills is supplied by waste biomass from the timber and paper industries at pricing equal or below conventional power sources.

This paper examines a UK business called Wind Direct, which installs and operates wind turbines at UK industrial sites, allowing its customers substantial savings on their overall electricity costs and reducing electricity pricing volatility.

Wind Direct Overview

Wind Direct is a business established in 2004 specifically to allow UK industries and other businesses with large electricity consumption to benefit from purchasing electricity directly from wind turbines located on their business premises. Customers can expect 10-20% savings on annual electric bills over current prices.

Wind Direct is owned by Wind Prospect Limited, one of the UK's leading wind farm development companies; Econnect, the leading electrical engineering company providing solutions for connecting wind turbines and other renewable projects to electric grids, Optimum Energy, a specialist in industrial power sales; and HgCapital, a London-based private equity firm with over a 20 year history.

Business Model and Customer Profile

Wind Direct offers customers long-term, fixed price power in return for installing, at Wind Direct's cost, wind turbines on UK industrial sites. Wind Direct offers a 100% lifetime outsourcing solution, including:

- Site evaluation, including suitability for wind turbines and wind resource;
- All costs of developing and permitting the site and installing and

operating the wind turbines;

- Evaluation of the customer's site electrical infrastructure and wind turbine connection requirements top ensure no interruption in electricity supply;
- Obtaining all planning consents and other permits to erect and operate the turbines;
- Interface with the customer's main electricity supplier to provide supplemental power;
- Turbine procurement and construction, including all related equipment;
- Connecting the turbines to the customer's site electric system;
- Turbine operations and maintenance; and
- Sales of green certificates generated by the wind turbines, which are the primary source of Wind Direct's profit.

The Benefits

Customers receive four key benefits: 10-20% savings on annual electricity bills; reduced power price volatility; enhanced sustainable or green image, and a 100% outsourced, no cost solution.

Cost Savings. Because there are no fuel costs, and wind turbine operating costs are very predictable, Wind Direct offers fixed price contracts for 10 years and beyond. These contracts are substantially below the current price of power from the grid. The lower cost is also driven by the fact that the customer does not need to pay (i) the mark-up that utilities charge on power from the grid and (ii) because the wind turbines are connected directly to the customer's internal grid, there are no transmission and distribution costs. As wind turbines do not operate at full output 100% of the time (the UK average is about 30%), depending on the customer's electricity requirements and the wind at the site, the power generated by the wind turbines will translate to a 10-20% annual cost savings.

Reduced Price Volatility. Grid power prices can be very volatile, with prices varying during the time of day (e.g. power prices are highest on cold winter days when more expensive units run and lower on summer weekends when there is relatively little demand) and with the cost of fuel. In the UK, natural gas is the predominant fuel for power generation. With the UK a net importer of gas, and gas prices linked to oil prices, pricing varies with the price of gas. The cost of wind does not vary with time, or with fuel prices, so it can reduce the volatility of annual power prices. The long-term contracts offered by Wind Direct allow customers to reduce the impact of this linkage and better forecast long-term energy costs.

Sustainable/Green Image. With corporate and social responsibility of increasing importance, there is no more visible demonstration of a proactive approach than an on-site wind turbine. The green "badge" can be fully exploited by the client even though they do not actually own the turbines.

100% Outsourced Solution. Many companies are exploring installing wind turbines themselves. This, however, takes time, expertise and capital. Wind Direct provides a 100% outsourced solution, including financing, at no cost to the customer. Wind Direct is experienced in securing planning consents, designing and constructing wind installations and operations. The customer need not devote staff time or capital resources to these complex tasks. This frees up capital and human resource for core business activities, whilst securing long-term cost savings.

Site Requirements
In addition to the electrical demand, the customers' sites should possess most, if not all of the following attributes:

- Sufficient land to allow the installation of 1-2 turbines at least 100-200 meters from any tall structures on the site.
- Ability to connect into the customer's internal electric grid.
- Residential areas at least 300-400 meters from the proposed wind turbines.
- Potential wind resource (e.g. not located at the very bottom of a step valley or dale).
- Away from major airports or MOD radar installations.

With these basic parameters, and a site layout, Wind Direct can quickly assess the viability of the site and potential customer savings.

Conclusion
Onsite wind generation can, contrary to many popularly held beliefs about renewable energy, generate cost savings for major energy users. Wind Direct, through its business model, offers customers a 100% outsourced solution. Though Wind Direct's creative use of the UK's renewable energy scheme, it achieves a "win-win" solution for clients.

Wind Direct Information
www.wind-direct.co.uk

Frances Davison
+44 (0)121 704 7123
frances.davison@windprospect.com

Other options available to businesses include shared savings schemes and leasing arrangements. Examples of this include facilities management companies offering energy management within a package of services. The cost of investment in resources and equipment is recovered by the facilities management company through the reduction in energy bills. Any residual savings can be passed on to the business client.

Similarly, some combined heat and power (CHP) companies provide third-party financing, recovering the initial outlay through charging for the electricity generated. The business client has a reduced rate for electricity without having to spend any capital.

Conclusion

Sustainable energy savings are not always a quick fix. Therefore, businesses need to take action now to improve their energy performance and optimize future energy budgets. Energy management has been too low on the priority scale for many businesses for too long. Upward pressures on the cost of energy and environmental awareness should encourage them to begin using it more efficiently. Reducing consumption is not as difficult as it may seem, and there are many solutions on the market that can help UK industry improve its performance. It simply needs to take the initiative.

Office efficiency

Anna Francis, Waste Watch

Making your office as sustainable and efficient as possible has commercial benefits and can entail significant cost savings. It also helps to improve an organization's profile and hence competitive advantage, and can increase staff morale. Taking control of the way your office uses resources improves management control as well as ensuring that your organization complies with legislation. Responsible environmental practice makes good business sense and is synonymous with a well-managed organization.

This chapter will examine four main areas of office efficiency: waste and recycling, equipment, energy use, and management systems that empower the workforce.

Waste and recycling

The way an organization uses and disposes of resources has an impact on both costs and the environment. Waste reduction at source – that is, careful purchasing to prevent waste – is environmentally and commercially the best option and is a growing area of business interest for many organizations. Waste is a commercial issue: the less waste you create, the less you pay to have it removed. Maximizing the efficiency of resources, such as printing double-sided, also means that less money is spent on procurement. Savings in waste disposal costs through reduction, reuse or recycling (see the hierarchy shown in Figure 5.3.1) can be particularly significant, and costs of waste disposal often tend to be underestimated, despite their recent substantial increase with the introduction of the landfill tax. Many companies do not know what they spend on waste, and few companies are aware that the real cost of waste (including the value

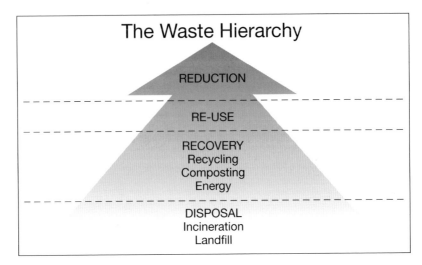

Source: Wastebusters Ltd, June 1996

Figure 5.3.1   Savings in waste disposal costs: the waste hierarchy

of raw materials, energy and wasted labour) can be up to 20 times the cost of disposal alone. On average, 70 per cent of office waste is recyclable, so there is significant potential for savings on disposal costs, although there will generally also be a fee for a recycling service.

In the United Kingdom each year the average office worker produces more than two and a half times his or her own body weight in rubbish. That's over 2 million tonnes across the United Kingdom. To take paper as an example, the average UK office employee uses nearly 15,000 sheets of A4 paper, the equivalent of one tree's worth of paper every year. It costs around £30 a tonne and rising to dispose of 'waste paper', yet the paper can be worth far more if it is sorted and recycled. Offices are potentially a major source of high-quality sorted waste papers. More than half of all office waste is made up of paper, most of which is high-grade white paper, the most sought-after type for recycling.

There are also significant environmental savings to be made by recycling. On average, the production of recycled paper involves between 28 per cent and 70 per cent less energy than producing virgin paper. Producing recycled paper saves (for 25,000 sheets of A4 paper) 17 trees, 7,000 gallons of water and 4,200 kilowatt-hours of electricity (enough for an average house for six months), and also reduces emissions of carbon dioxide and nitrogen.

What can be recycled?

The following common office wastes can be recycled:

- paper;
- cardboard;
- computers and related components;

- toner and ink cartridges;
- office equipment, eg photocopiers;
- mobile phones;
- fluorescent light tubes;
- furniture;
- batteries.

Waste generated by catering services can also be recycled:

- aluminium cans and foil;
- cooking oils;
- glass;
- plastic bottles;
- plastic cups from vending machines.

Fruit, vegetable peelings, tea bags and coffee grounds can also potentially be composted.

Options for an office recycling service

There are a number of collection options when selecting a recycling contractor to service an office, each of which requires different levels of staff involvement, space and frequency of collection. As a result of these factors, the quality of the material collected for recycling will also vary. Staff engagement is important, as the more staff an organization has, the more waste it will produce, which therefore increases the amount of material available for recycling.

Moving office

Moving to a new office can create a significant amount of waste as well as offering opportunities for more efficient waste management in the future. However, unwanted office furniture can now be reused and recycled (see http://www.frn.org.uk/code/find/map.asp for details), and, when setting up a new office, recycling facilities can be installed at suitably convenient points to encourage staff to recycle and maximize the effectiveness of the scheme.

How do I start recycling?

The following are suggestions for how to start:

- Know what waste you are producing and identify what materials you think could be recycled.
- Identify recycling collection contractors in your area.
- Gain senior management commitment.
- Engage the support of other contractors, such as cleaners and interested staff, in implementing a system.

- Agree a recycling plan, highlighting when schemes will be introduced, reviewed and expanded.
- Once the infrastructure is in place, run an internal awareness-raising campaign to encourage staff to recycle, and use this as a way of developing 'green teams' or 'recycling champions'.
- Ask your recycling contractor to record and provide you with information on the quantity of material that you have recycled. Use these data to highlight the positive impact of staff actions and to improve capture rates (ie the percentage of a potentially recyclable material that is actually collected for recycling).
- Include information on recycling in staff induction programmes and the staff handbook, and encourage staff feedback.
- Buy recycled products.

Barriers to recycling and how to overcome them

The main barriers to recycling are:

- space restrictions;
- lack of available recycling services in your area;
- minimum quantities of material required for collection;
- cost of collection of material(s) for recycling or of the implementation of a scheme;
- lack of staff engagement or understanding.

However, good planning, endorsed schemes, reviewed action and good communication with contractors and staff will help to overcome these barriers and will help you keep up to date with legislative changes and changes in service provision.

What is considered to be best practice in office recycling and reduction? The answer is a recycling rate of 70 per cent and a figure of 200 kilograms of waste production per full-time-equivalent member of staff.

If you recycle your waste, it is also important that you buy recycled products ('closing the loop'); unless there are viable markets, recycling is not always cost-effective. For more information about recycled products, see www.recycledproducts.org.uk.

Legislation and regulation

It is essential to comply with legislation and regulations that govern waste disposal, including:

- the Environmental Protection Act 1990, including the Duty of Care Regulations;
- the Environment Act 1995;
- the Landfill Directive;
- the Packaging and Packaging Waste Directive;
- the Waste Electronic and Electronic Equipment (WEEE) Directive.

For further information, contact:

■ the Environment Agency for England and Wales, www.environment-agency.gov.
   uk;
■ the Scottish Environmental Protection Agency, www.sepa.org.uk;
■ the Northern Ireland Environment and Heritage Service, www.ehsni.gov.uk/
   default.asp.

Equipment

The choice and management of office equipment can have a huge impact on both
the environmental and the organizational costs of an office. How long a piece of
equipment lasts, the energy and resources it uses and the way it is disposed of are
all significant. While energy use for the heating and lighting of offices is decreasing
and becoming more efficient, the energy used by office equipment continues to rise.
In fact, office equipment is the fastest-growing user of energy in the business world,
and electricity consumption by office equipment now represents 25 per cent of total
electrical energy use in offices. Its impact on the environment (and an organization's
costs) is therefore considerable. For example, carbon dioxide (CO_2) emissions arising
from such consumption are a major contributor to climate change. Furthermore,
because of the limited life of most office equipment, substantial waste is produced
when equipment is finally disposed of.

Fortunately, there is now an extensive range of environmentally preferable
products that can reduce your costs and environmental impact. These products are
often no more expensive to purchase and are usually cheaper to operate. Preference
should be given to energy-efficient equipment and equipment that reduces resource
use (and hence costs), such as printers that can print double-sided and photocopiers
that have easy-to-use duplex settings.

Staff awareness and understanding of their impacts in relation to office equipment
use are also key to successfully reducing the environmental and cost implications of
equipment use, for example making employees aware of the benefits of turning off
their computer monitors if they are away from their desks.

Energy

Office energy bills can often be reduced by 10–20 per cent by introducing a range of
measures, many of which involve little or no expenditure. For example:

■ Energy-efficient light bulbs last six times as long as conventional types and cost
   one-tenth as much to run.
■ Reducing the temperature of your office by 1 °C will reduce your fuel bill by 10
   per cent.
■ If you do not service your boiler for one year, its efficiency can drop by 10 per
   cent.

- A photocopier left switched on overnight uses enough energy to make 5,300 A4 copies.
- A PC monitor uses 80 per cent of a PC's energy. If you are away from your desk for more than 30 minutes, it is more cost-effective to switch your PC monitor off. A monitor left switched on overnight uses enough energy to laser-print 800 A4 pages.
- Lighting an empty office overnight uses enough energy to heat water for 1,000 cups of coffee. Even if you are leaving your office for only 5 or 10 minutes, it is still more cost-effective to switch off your lights.

When purchasing office equipment, it is important to consider whole-life energy cost savings; it may save you money in the longer term to pay more initially. For example, over its lifespan a fluorescent tube will save 640 kilowatt-hours of electricity compared with the equivalent 100-watt standard bulb. This reduces the production of carbon dioxide, a greenhouse gas, by half a tonne and that of sulphur dioxide, which causes acid rain, by 3 kilograms. Preference should be given to equipment that has the Energy Efficiency Recommended logo or a similar standard. When purchasing new equipment, ask your suppliers for information on the average power consumed under normal operating conditions. You could then develop that information into a more formal green procurement policy, establishing a policy of purchasing energy-saving equipment and making it a requirement that the lifetime cost of new equipment is included in the purchasing decision. Once the equipment is purchased, it is important to make sure that the 'power save' feature is activated, as equipment is often set up with it disabled.

How to start greening your office

The most effective approach to setting up a green office is to involve senior management from the beginning, as it is much easier to get things done when an effort has the backing of management. A signed commitment from senior management towards improving the environmental performance of your organization is a good start. This commitment could then potentially be developed into an environmental policy: a written statement outlining an organization's main environmental impacts and aims in relation to managing these impacts. In the absence of senior management commitment, individuals and groups of employees can still achieve significant environmental improvements.

Assign responsibilities

Nominating individuals to take responsibility for a particular environmental improve-ment is very important, as they can ensure that the changes needed are followed through. Setting up an informal committee to coordinate efforts and share information is also very beneficial. Encouraging in-house suggestions and rewarding initiatives or innovation in the context of recycling can also help to create a successful green office.

Review current performance and collect data

Reviewing existing practice means that opportunities for environmental improvements can easily be identified. It involves examining resource use, energy and water use, transport, procurement, and current waste disposal methods. By collecting baseline data on energy and water consumption and on waste production, future improvements can be compared. This can be done internally or with the help of external consultants.

Set priorities

Improving the environmental performance of your organization is a long-term project. Some changes will take longer and require more resources to implement than others. However, there are lots of things that can be done straight away, such as setting up a paper recycling scheme, so this could be prioritized while more complicated changes could be undertaken later.

Eventually you may feel that the organization needs a more formal approach to improving its environmental performance. Longer-term changes can be incorporated into an environmental management system (EMS), which can be independently audited if required.

Communicate and promote

Communication is central to improving efficiency and environmental performance. Ensuring that everyone understands what you want to do, why and how and that they receive regular feedback on targets and achievements can help to ensure continued interest and involvement. Formulating and then communicating an environmental policy is also useful and is key to developing and implementing an EMS. An environmental policy allows an organization to communicate its environmental aims and objectives to employees, shareholders, customers, suppliers and any other interested parties.

Review and improve

In a green office, concern for the environment should be an integral part of everyday operations. Environmental improvement is an ongoing process, and new products and processes are constantly being developed. The best way of maintaining and improving a green office is to establish a more formal EMS, which will put in place a continual process of review and improvement.

Environmental management systems

Adopting a more formal approach through implementing an EMS has a number of advantages. Integrating responsibility for environmental issues into day-to-day work ensures that initiatives last beyond initial enthusiasm. An EMS also helps organizations to identify all their environmental effects and potential risks in a structured and systematic way rather than responding to outside pressures on an ad hoc basis. In addition, as more organizations adopt EMSs, they are starting to look at the effect their supply chain has on the environment. By implementing environmental measures, you can comply with your customers' requirements and be in a better position to win EMS-registered clients.

Environmental management system standards

The main EMS standard is ISO 14001. There is also a European regulation, the Eco-Management and Audit Scheme (EMAS). These management standards have created an international blueprint for integrating environmental issues into the management structure of an organization. They are not the only possible designs for an environmental management system, but they do provide an opportunity for independent certification of an organization's commitment to responsible environmental practice. For more information, see http://emea.bsi-global.com/Environment/.

Waste Watch Environmental Consultancy

Waste Watch Environmental Consultancy (WWEC, formerly Wastebusters) provides practical support to businesses wishing to implement efficient and cost-effective sound environmental practice. Our client list features high-profile organizations from both the public and the private sector, and we can help you with:

- resource management;
- waste audits;
- green procurement policies;
- waste minimization plans;
- environmental reporting;
- education and awareness-raising programmes;
- advice on sustainable transport;
- feasibility studies;
- composting research.

WWEC/Wastebusters also compiled the *Green Office Manual*, which provides businesses of all sizes with clear, jargon-free, concise information about environmental issues and the practical steps that can be taken to create a green office environment. It highlights the opportunities for achieving cost savings through environmental improvements and sets out effective, simple mechanisms to encourage participation and commitment from staff and suppliers.

Waste Watch Environmental Consultancy is managed by Waste Watch Services, the trading arm of Waste Watch (www.wastewatch.org.uk), the national charity promoting waste reduction, reuse and recycling. For more information about WWEC, see www.wastebusters.co.uk.

Thames Water and climate change

Richard Aylard, Thames Water

Summary

Thames Water is the UK's largest water company, serving over 13 million customers in London and the Thames Valley, from Kent and Essex in the east to the edge of Gloucestershire in the west. We look after a large infrastructure network with some 60,000 miles of water and sewerage pipes – enough to run around the world twice.

Climate change will produce greater extremes of weather, such as drier summers and wetter winters. This will pose serious problems for our operations, whether providing water or disposing of sewage. Drier summers will mean increased demand at the same time as river flows fall, affecting our ability to supply water. Lower river flows resulting in reduced capacity may create problems for sewage treatment.

The challenge for Thames Water and its regulators is to find solutions that balance competing environmental, social and economic demands in a sustainable and integrated way. Climate change cannot be thought about in isolation. It must be integrated into our business planning, operations, finance and regulation. Thames Water has made a start responding to these issues – but we need to do more.

Change the climate in your business

There has been a sustained period of drought since November 2004 in the South East of England and we need your help to save water.

Water bills could cost your company over 1% of its turnover and it's possible to achieve savings on these with a few simple steps.

For water saving information, visit our website at www.thameswater.co.uk/waterwise

Introduction

Climate change is already having an impact. In August 2003, Brogdale in Kent experienced the UK's highest-ever recorded temperature – 38.5 °C. November that year saw rainfall rise to 183 per cent of the historical monthly average – a significant increase. These are not isolated incidents – the last decade of the 20th century was the warmest for 100 years (Met Office, 2003) – and evidence suggests rainfall patterns are changing and will continue to do so (see Figure 5.4.1).[1]

Thames Water is highly dependent on the natural environment – one reason why it is heavily regulated.[2] It borrows water from the environment, treats it and supplies it to customers. It collects and treats wastewater and returns it to the environment. Changes such as reduced rainfall are therefore a very serious issue for the business.

The South-East of England is already water-stressed (Entec, 2002). The hot, dry summer of 2003 saw reservoir levels fall to as low as 40 per cent of capacity.[3] Restrictions were avoided only because of the lessons learnt from previous droughts.[4]

Government position

Climate change is the world's greatest environmental challenge.

(Prime Minister Tony Blair, September 2004)

In my view, climate change is the most severe problem we are facing today, more serious even than the threat of terrorism.

(Sir David King, UK Chief Scientist, 2004)

The UK government has explicitly stated that it expects water companies and regulators to deal with climate change in a sensible way, which neither ignores risks nor is over-precautionary (Defra, 2003).[5] Tony Blair and Sir David King have since strengthened the government's position. This means that, regardless of scientific debates over the causes of climate change, Thames Water must take it into account in its business planning and operations.

Climate change and Thames Water

Regional studies of climate change impacts, *A Climate Change Impacts in London Evaluation Study* (Entec, 2002) and *Rising to the Challenge* (WS Atkins, 1999) have shown that water and wastewater issues will be critical factors in the South-East. The impacts must be considered in relation both to our statutory duties to provide safe water and dispose of effluents and to the environment we work within.

Thames Water must therefore ask five questions:

1. What is climate change and what will the future climate be like?
2. What are the potential impacts on Thames Water?[6]
3. What could these impacts mean for the business?[7]

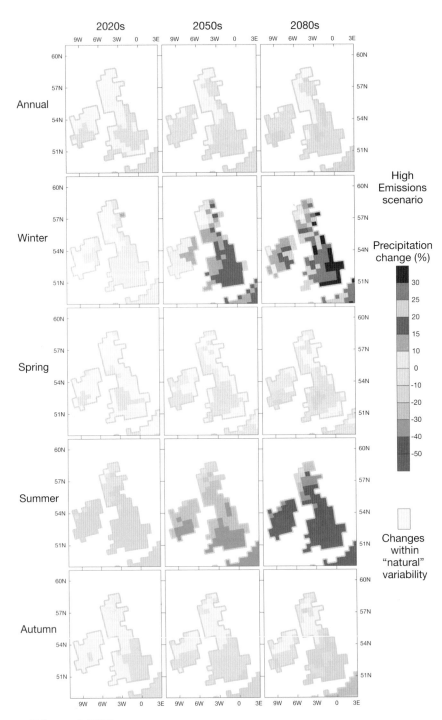

Source: Hulme et al (2002)

Figure 5.4.1 Changes in precipitation to 2080

4. What is Thames Water already doing to adapt to and mitigate the impacts of climate change?
5. How can Thames Water strategically respond to the challenge of climate change?[8]

Q1 – What is climate change and what will the future climate be like?

The climate is changing as a consequence of the emission of greenhouse gases. In less than two centuries, the concentration of these gases has increased by 50 per cent compared to pre-industrial revolution levels (Hulme *et al*, 2002). The consequences are already being felt, according to the Intergovernmental Panel on Climate Change, the most authoritative scientific and technical voice on the subject. These impacts will inevitably increase over the next 100 years because of the inertia of our climate system.[9]

What this means for the UK is demonstrated by four scenarios in Figure 5.4.2 produced by the United Kingdom Climate Impacts Programme (UKCIP), based on different assumptions about world development and therefore greenhouse gas levels.[10] Under the medium-high scenario, a hot August like that of 1995 when the average temperature was 3.4 °C above the average between 1961 and 1990 will occur twice every three years by the 2080s. A dry summer like that of 1995, which was 37 per cent drier than average, will occur every other year by the 2080s.

	Anomaly	2020s	2050s	2080s
Mean				
A hot '1995-type' year	3.4 °C	1%	20%	63%
A warm '1999-type' year	1.2 °C	28%	73%	100%
Precipitation				
A dry '1995-type' summer	37% drier	10%	29%	50%
A wet '1994/95-type' winter	66%	1%	3%	7%

Source: Hulme *et al* (2002)

Figure 5.4.2   Percentage of years experiencing various extreme seasonal anomalies across central England and Wales for the medium-high scenario relative to the 1961–90 climate

Clearly, if this happens there will be significant impacts on the amount of water in the natural environment available to be supplied to the public. Demand for water would also increase during warm periods (Hulme *et al*, 2002).

It is also likely that seasonal weather patterns will change, which will see spring temperatures occurring between one and three weeks earlier than now and longer growing seasons. Both will increase the demands for water by consumers, agriculture and the natural environment.

Q2 – What are the potential impacts on Thames Water?

Figure 5.4.3 shows the company's activities.

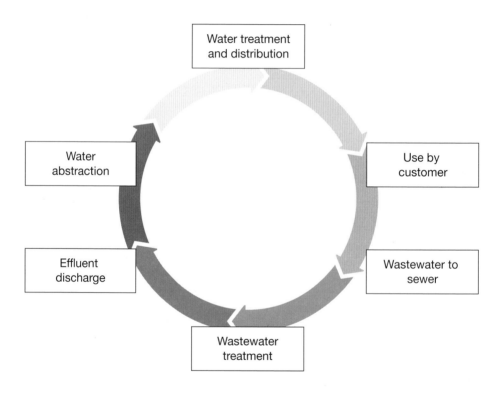

Figure 5.4.3   Thames Water's activities

Thames Water has carried out a study that has identified a wide range of potential issues where the organization may be at risk if it does not adapt these activities (Colquhoun, 2004). These include:

■   reduced water availability and quality;
■   impacts on the robustness and serviceability of assets;

- threats to assets from floods;
- change in demand patterns, notably increased demand in summer;
- changes in the pattern and frequency of droughts;
- increased frequency and intensity of rainfall leading to more foul flooding;
- increased variability in volume and strength of sewage throughout the year, affecting the efficiency of wastewater treatment plants;
- reduced ability of the natural environment to dilute treated effluent;
- regulator and customer expectations such as the sustainability of existing services;
- maintaining environmental standards against a backdrop of potentially conflicting issues such as mitigating climate change and improving effluent standards;
- risk – uncertainty over the varying climate scenarios means uncertainty over design specifications, new regulations and financial models to be adopted;
- health and safety – our street gangs may need extra protection such as sun-screening protective clothing.

Q3 - What could these impacts mean for the business?

What future are we planning for?

Unlike most business sectors, the water industry must plan for the long term of 25 years or more (many assets such as reservoirs or pipes last over 100 years). Our water resources planning has a 25-year horizon, yet the five-year regulatory planning cycles make strategic planning difficult. Instead, they focus on short-term deliverables, and immediate political and financial imperatives mean that more strategic considerations tend to suffer.

The 2004 Periodic Price Review allowed companies to address climate change in their business plans. Although government support was limited, this was a step in the right direction. It is hoped future reviews will encourage more long-term planning, especially given recent government statements committing the government to taking a lead on climate change.

Such difficulties are compounded by the uncertainties about the future climate and therefore how to plan ahead over issues such as design standards.

Issues with standards

The Victorians had not heard of climate change when they designed the sewers we still use today. Forecast wetter winters and extreme wet weather events are likely to overload the network more often, leading to more local flooding. The industry, led by Thames Water, has looked at this issue through a three-year research project. However, this raised more questions than answers.

Many of Thames Water's treatment works and abstraction and effluent discharge points are located on rivers and are often on flood plains. They will therefore be more at risk of being damaged or cut off by floods. Relocation is usually unfeasible, but it is unclear what design solutions to adopt.

To meet increased demand in drier summers, it will be necessary to capture more rainwater falling in the wetter winters. This means more upstream reservoir capacity. Continued regulatory resistance to this solution means such a reservoir may not be online in time if climate change is at the drier end of possible futures. This would be a real risk to the business and its stakeholders.[11]

Potential impacts

A number of significant potential impacts on Thames Water's activities have been identified:

- Increased flooding and soil moisture content will lead to greater infiltration of water into the sewerage network, resulting in more dilute sewage. Conversely, drier summers and higher temperatures will result in more concentrated sewage that is likely to require additional treatment. Sewage treatment works will therefore be required to operate under a wide range of conditions, both in summer and in winter.
- Reduced dilution in low-flow rivers may lead to a ratcheting up of effluent standards. Technical retro-fit solutions at many plants are limited by space constraints and tend to be very energy-intensive, contributing to increased greenhouse gas emissions. The overall environmental impact must be considered – how should river quality be balanced against future climate damage in the interests of true sustainability?
- Thames Water has statutory duties to enhance conservation, access and recreation. Climate change could lead to climate belts moving northwards. Chalk streams in the South-East could dry up, and temperature increases could lead to a loss of protected species, regardless of how the organization operates (Spillett, 2004).
- Climate change could mean fewer burst pipes as a result of fewer cold spells. But its impact on London's clay soil is expected to lead to more soil movement, potentially increasing the damage to pipes in the area. This would compound Thames Water's already difficult leakage problem.
- Continued investment in water and wastewater services will be necessary to allow us to continue to meet the current and future levels of service expected by Ofwat and customers.

Q4 – What is Thames Water already doing to adapt to and mitigate the impacts of climate change?

The challenge for Thames Water and its regulators – environmental and economic – is to balance often competing demands to ensure that sustainable and integrated solutions are found. Providing enough water for customers' needs and effectively disposing of sewage whilst protecting the environment will require a sustainable balance between customer and regulatory demands.

We are committed to reducing our greenhouse gas emissions through good energy management and development of renewable energy sources. We have reported our emissions since 1997 and these have fallen by 15 per cent between 1990 and 2004, despite the need to build and operate new processes.

We have built climate change forecasts into our operational and strategic planning – such as applying the UKCIP scenarios to our modelling work for the 2005–10 Strategic Business Plan and our latest Water Resources Plan. However, we want to do more.

To achieve this, Thames Water has:

■ assessed the potential impacts and issues climate change may present;
■ developed a climate change policy;
■ begun a programme to stabilize greenhouse gas emissions;
■ improved energy efficiency and third-party accreditation;
■ begun work to increase significantly the level of self-generated renewable electricity;
■ committed to managing existing resources as effectively as possible, and to looking at and developing new sustainable water resource solutions;
■ continued to influence customer demand through water efficiency campaigns;
■ worked with stakeholders such as the London Climate Change Partnership and the South-East Climate Change Partnerships to embed water efficiency in guidance documents such as 'Adapting to climate change: a checklist for developers';
■ started to further embed climate change issues in its business decision making to ensure we effectively plan for the future.

We are already working proactively with many stakeholders, including the Environment Agency, the Greater London Authority, the Government Office for London, Defra, and the London and South-East Climate Change Partnerships, to research and share understanding of the impacts of climate change on the whole water cycle. Together, we seek to ensure that adaptation and mitigation responses are sustainable and fair for all.

Q5 – How can Thames Water strategically respond to the challenge of climate change?

Thames Water embraces sustainable development, as we believe it is key to ensuring a better quality of life, now and for generations to come. We must respond to climate change to ensure that our activities make a positive contribution to the wider goal of achieving sustainable development. The anticipated impact of climate change in South-East England will compound an already difficult situation in an area where water resources are already stressed. Not only do we need to reduce our greenhouse gas emissions, but we must work proactively to manage our adaptation responses in a sustainable and equitable way.

We have made good progress in areas such as water resources planning and energy efficiency. However, there are areas where our progress is not as advanced. For example, our understanding and response concerning our sewerage system design and operation are far more limited.

We have identified the need for a central climate change strategy spelling out clearly what is expected of the business and its employees if we are to achieve our goal of responding effectively. A number of key areas have been identified that we need to address as we develop this strategy:

■ The strategy cannot exist in isolation. To deliver tangible results, it must be integrated with and build upon current policies and strategies such as corporate responsibility, water resources, wastewater management, energy, environmental purchasing, transport, waste reduction and recycling.
■ Positive progress, both internally and externally, will depend on improving communication and understanding to change behaviours and culture.
■ It is imperative we engage with stakeholders and regulators to share understanding and learn about each other's climate change issues and concerns.

Conclusions

The environment and sustainability will be a central focus of the organization in the future, particularly the quality of discharged effluent to protect river quality, drinking water quality to ensure public health, reduction of greenhouse gas emissions to save energy and protect the environment, and minimizing waste to conserve natural resources. Within Thames Water, this commitment to the environment is more than just rhetoric and is backed up by action and transparent reporting (Thames Water, 2005).

The water industry in the UK and around the world is highly regulated and becoming more so. This regulation impacts upon all aspects of our operations, from the quality of drinking water supplied to customers to the quality of effluent returned to the environment, the requirement to develop long-term plans over 25 years, sustainability, protecting and improving the environment and what we charge our customers for the services we provide.

Thames Water believes that environmental protection and increasing corporate value are not mutually opposing goals but are interrelated. Companies that act in an environmentally and socially responsible manner are more successful in the market over the long run. Capital markets are increasingly interested in knowing how companies meet these responsibilities. That is why analysts, the world over, are continually looking at our commitment in the areas of sustainability, environmental management and response to issues such as climate change. In addition, our customers expect innovative, environmentally safe solutions.

We know we cannot deliver the necessary responses and solutions required to meet the challenges climate change presents without working closely with regulators, stakeholders and the wider public.

Notes

1   Figure 5.4.1 shows the percentage change in annual winter and summer precipitation for the time slices of the 2020s, 2050s and 2080s for two different

UKCIP02 scenarios – low and high. They show that the amount of rainfall, particularly in the South-East, will significantly reduce both annually and in summer. Only in winter will it rise.

2 We have three main regulators – the Environment Agency, Ofwat (the financial regulator) and the Drinking Water Inspectorate.

3 In an average year, reservoir levels would typically be 90 per cent full by November.

4 The droughts of 1976 and 1995 led to better resource planning processes that are coupled with extensive drought management plans, which can be implemented during very dry spells.

5 The Secretary of State for the Environment, Food and Rural Affairs set out guidance to Ofwat and therefore water companies about how to consider in a sustainable way: 1) the security and safety of water supplies; 2) water and sewerage services in a way that respects the environment; and 3) the furtherance of social and economic policies with respect to the five-year Periodic Price Review PR-04.

6 This includes components such as the environmental, social, political, economic, technological and demographic.

7 How can we adapt to these changes, which we cannot prevent, and how can we reduce or mitigate longer-term impacts?

8 How can climate change be incorporated into the strategic thinking of Thames Water at board level?

9 The climate has many components, which respond on different timescales. When increases in greenhouse emissions lead to an imbalance between incoming energy from the sun and outgoing energy from the earth there is a net flow of heat into the atmosphere. If greenhouse gas emissions are stabilized, the climate system will gradually warm until a new balance is found at a higher temperature. Although the atmosphere responds relatively quickly, the oceans and ice caps respond much more slowly. Consequently, changes are inevitable for the next 100 years – even if we stabilized emissions immediately.

10 UKCIP was set up in 1997 by the government to provide a framework for an assessment of climate change impacts. It helps organizations identify how they will be affected so they can plan how to adapt.

11 Reducing leakage will help, but it is not a long-term solution in itself. The region will be in water deficit by the 2020s regardless of climate change impacts. Building a reservoir takes about 20 years, so we need to start soon.

References

Colquhoun, KO (2004) Climate change and its potential impact on Thames Water: issues and strategic options, MBS thesis, University of Derby

Department for Environment, Food and Rural Affairs (Defra) (2003) *Initial Guidance from the Secretary of State to the Director-General of Water Services: 2004 periodic review of water prices*, Defra, London

Entec (2002) *A Climate Change Impacts in London Evaluation Study*, GLA, London

Hulme, M *et al* (2002) *Climate Change Scenarios for the United Kingdom: The UKCIP02 scientific report*, Tyndall Centre for Climate Change Research, School of Environmental Sciences, University of East Anglia, Norwich

King, D (2004) Climate change science: adapt, mitigate or ignore?, *Science*, **303**, pp 176–77

Met Office (2003) *2003: Fifth warmest year in Britain*, http://www.metoffice.gov.uk/cgi-bin/printpage.cgi (accessed 20 February 2004)

Spillett, PB (2004) Policy perspectives for the water industry, Presented at EA/Defra workshop: What we need to know and when – decision-makers' perspective on climate change science, 16–17 February 2004, Birmingham University

Thames Water (2005) *Corporate Responsibility Report 2004*, Thames Water, Reading

WS Atkins (1999) *Rising to the Challenge: Impacts of climate change in the South East in the 21st century*, WS Atkins, Oxford

Tackling climate change globally

Unilever

The Unilever strategy

Unilever believes that one of the best and most sustainable ways it can help to address global social and environmental concerns is through the very business of doing business in a socially aware and responsible manner. Across the spectrum of its food, home and personal care products and their distribution across the world – in Africa, Europe, Asia, Australasia and the Americas – Unilever practises what it preaches. Its consumer brands include Dove, Sunsilk, Rexona, Omo, Cif, Lipton, Knorr, Hellmann's, Becel/Flora, Bertolli and ice creams such as Magnum and Cornetto.

Unilever's environmental strategy focuses on six goals. The company's sustainability initiatives in agriculture, fish and water target areas that are directly relevant to the company and, in partnership with others, work towards ensuring a sustainable supply of key resources. Eco-innovation improves the impacts of its products and eco-efficiency in manufacturing – making more with less – reduces the impacts of its own operations. Essential elements of its eco-efficiency programme include improving energy efficiency in manufacturing, reducing emissions, and the introduction of climate-friendly hydrocarbon refrigerants in its retail freezer cabinets.

Unilever's carbon dioxide emissions from energy use in manufacturing have dropped consistently, and since 1995 Unilever has achieved reductions of 31 per cent on a per-tonne-of-production basis.

Addressing global warming

Global warming brings unpredictable environmental consequences for society and business. Professor Dan Esty, director of the Yale Center for Environmental Law and Policy, is an adviser to Unilever on the environment. Warning that global warming threatens the company's key sources of ingredients – agriculture and fisheries – he has said that 'Unilever could be vulnerable to changes in global temperature, sea level, rainfall patterns, soil moisture and storm patterns.'

Refrigeration

Unilever has made significant progress in the area of refrigeration. For industrial-scale refrigeration, all of its ice cream and frozen foods factories use ammonia, which does not contribute to global warming or ozone depletion. For retail refrigeration, Unilever is replacing ice cream freezer cabinets using HFCs with more climate-friendly hydrocarbon (HC) refrigerants. The HC technology has been developed in close cooperation with Greenpeace and was launched in Europe, where the number of HC cabinets will reach 100,000 in 2006. Roll-out in other parts of the world is under way or planned. The HC cabinets are also more energy-efficient and use up to 9 per cent less energy than older technologies. Stephen Tindale, UK executive director of Greenpeace, supports Unilever's actions and, commenting at the time on the company's award-winning 2005 performance, said that 'Unilever has shown genuine commitment to the environment and genuine business leadership. This sends a powerful message to the rest of industry that climate-friendly technology is available and must now be used.'

Manufacturing eco-efficiency

Unilever's performance in improving its manufacturing eco-efficiency and specifically its CO_2 emissions from energy use are detailed in Table 5.5.1.

Table 5.5.1   The global past trend and future targets in kilograms of CO_2 per tonne of production

	2001	2002	2003	2004	2005	Target 2006	Target 2010
CO_2	198.59	195.17	191.46	185.67	171.30	165.30	153.43

Energy consumption

In the United States the Home and Personal Care Division of Unilever cut energy use by over 10 per cent in a single year when in 2001 it began to publish energy costs for each site and encouraged internal competition to make savings. In the UK, Unilever's food business is aiming to beat targets set as part of the UK government's programme to raise energy awareness and improve efficiency.

As well as working to make its own operations more energy efficient, Unilever also aims to help consumers save energy when they use its products. For example, laundry detergents have been developed to work at low temperatures so that less energy is needed to heat the washing water.

Renewable energy

The use of renewable energy, such as solar, wind and biomass, can contribute to reducing emissions. Wood and other vegetation (biomass) are currently the main renewable fuels used by the company, followed by hydro- and wind electricity. In Unilever's case, 16.5 per cent of total energy consumption was provided from renewable sources in 2005 and in some places today renewables provide the main source of power.

For example, in India, around 80 per cent of the power used by the company's present and former tea estates was derived from wood. The factories there used to be powered by coal, but Unilever now grows trees, mainly eucalyptus, for wood burning in well-managed plantations. Burning wood only releases carbon taken from the air during growth so that there is no net impact on the atmosphere. Therefore, the process is carbon neutral.

In Kenya, 97 per cent of the energy used by Unilever's Kericho tea estates is provided by renewable sources, including both hydroelectricity and fuel wood. The estate has been working with Kenya Forestry Research Institute to increase the use of wood, improve yields and boost boiler efficiency.

In 2005, Unilever comfortably met its global target for reducing its unit energy load by 6.7 per cent, with a 4.9 per cent reduction in absolute energy. The company also achieved a 7.7 per cent reduction in load of CO_2 from energy per tonne of production and a 6.4 per cent reduction in absolute load.

Conclusion

Undoubtedly, much can be achieved by industry through individual company efforts to cut energy consumption. However, substantial progress towards combating climate change will only be made if business, government and all stakeholders work together.

The collaboration between Greenpeace and Unilever, which produced the HC cabinet programme that dampens the global warming effects from increased ice cream sales in warmer weather, is just one example of what can be achieved by working in partnership.

Emissions and contaminants: legal overview

Julie Smith, Simmons & Simmons

Legislation regulating the release of contaminants and other emissions into the environment is increasingly focusing on the desired result in terms of the quality of the environment. This is particularly true of recent and future legislation emerging at European level, and some examples illustrating this are given below.

The EU Emissions Trading Scheme began operation on 1 January 2005. The scheme covers carbon dioxide emissions from installations in the energy sector, ferrous metal sector, mineral industry, and those producing timber or other fibrous minerals or paper and board. The scheme works on a cap-and-trade basis, with member state governments setting an overall national cap consistent with Kyoto Protocol targets. The overall national allocation of allowances is divided between individual installations, which are required to present allowances equal to their emissions at the end of each compliance year. Preparations for Phase 2 of the scheme, which will run from 2008 until the end of 2012, are under way. Member states are required to submit draft national allocation plans to the Commission by the end of June 2006. In the meantime, the Commission is carrying out a review of the scheme and is expected to report on its review by the same date.

What sort of mother makes her child drink water like this?

WaterAid/Jeremy Horner

One that doesn't have any choice

Clean water is something that most of us take for granted, but over a billion people in the world don't have it and over two billion people lack basic sanitation. As a result a child dies every 15 seconds from water-related diseases.

WaterAid is the UK's only major charity dedicated exclusively to the provision of safe domestic water, sanitation and hygiene education to the world's poorest people. Our projects are set up by local organisations and managed by the community so that the benefits last long in to the future.

To find out more contact:

WaterAid, 47-49 Durham Street, London, SE11 5JD

020 7793 4500
www.wateraid.org

Charity registration number 288701

♂ WaterAid

Clean water is something we can take for granted but over a billion people in the world don't have it, and over two and a half billion people lack basic sanitation. As a result a child dies every 15 seconds from water-related diseases.

Without safe water and sanitation nearby people find it impossible to escape the downward spiral of poverty and disease. Many women and children in developing countries spend hours each day walking miles to collect water, taking up valuable time and energy, preventing women from working and stopping children from going to school. The water they walk so far to collect is usually dirty and unsafe, but they have no alternative.

WaterAid is the UK's only major charity dedicated exclusively to the provision of safe domestic water, sanitation and hygiene education to the world's poorest people. Since 1981 WaterAid has helped over 8.5 million people and now works in 17 countries in Africa, Asia and the Pacific region. With local organisations WaterAid helps to set up low cost, sustainable projects using appropriate technology. The local community is empowered to plan, construct, manage and maintain their own projects so that they last long into the future.

WaterAid also seeks to influence water and sanitation policies at a national and international level to ensure that more of the world's poorest people gain access to these basic needs.

As an independent charity WaterAid needs support to carry out this vital work. WaterAid can work with companies and individuals in a range of ways from high profile events, to long-term strategic partnerships or employee involvement.

Your support today will help expand our work to help more of world's poorest people gain access to safe water and a better quality of life.

Call 020 7793 4500 or visit www.wateraid.org to find out more.
Charity registration number 288701.

In a major change to the control of chemicals, the new REACH (Registration, Evaluation and Authorization of Chemicals) scheme is now at the advanced proposal stage and looks set to become law in early 2007. The scheme is partly an attempt to bring under legislative control those chemicals that escaped regulation owing to the length of time they have been on the market. It requires, among other things, more testing and information for most chemical substances, and erases the distinction between existing and new chemicals.

The Water Framework Directive (2000/60/EC) establishing a framework for Community action in the field of water policy was finally adopted in October 2000. It is the most substantial piece of EU water legislation to have been produced, protecting all waters – rivers, lakes, coastal waters and groundwaters – and setting objectives that will ensure they meet 'good status' by 2015. A draft Groundwater Directive aimed at protecting groundwaters has been proposed by the Commission and is expected to be adopted by the end of 2006. The proposed directive sets standards for 'good status' in relation to nitrates and pesticides and requires member states to set standards for other pollutants. Member states are also required to identify any significant and sustained upward trend in pollutants found in groundwater and reverse those trends that present a significant risk of harm to the quality of aquatic systems or terrestrial ecosystems, to human health or to actual or potential legitimate uses of the water environment. Finally, member states must take measures to prevent inputs to groundwater of hazardous substances and to limit the input of other pollutants.

As part of its Clean Air for Europe Programme (CAFE) the Commission has also proposed a new Air Quality Framework Directive that would revise and consolidate existing European law on air quality. The proposed directive would restate existing limit values and would set new limit values for fine particulates ($PM_{2.5}$). The new proposal allows a member state that has taken all reasonable measures to achieve compliance to be allowed additional time to achieve that compliance in respect of a particular zone or agglomeration provided that it has established an air pollution abatement programme setting out how standards will be achieved within the additional time allowed.

CLIMATE CARE

Climate Care raises funds by selling greenhouse gas emissions reductions (referred to as CO_2 offsets). It then develops projects that reduce emissions, ensuring that the total reductions achieved match the amounts sold.

Examples of the projects that Climate Care is funding include:

- Efficient coffee drying in Costa Rica – coffee farmers currently supplement their dryers with wood cut unsustainably from local forests. Climate Care is providing the equity to install efficient burners that eliminate the need for the wood

- Low energy lighting in low income households in South Africa – as electricity is generated from coal saving electricity reduces CO_2 emissions, as well as reducing bills for householders

- Reforestation in Uganda – substantial parts of Kibale National Park in Uganda were cut down in the 1970s. Climate Care is contributing to the replanting of the area with native tree species. As well as sequestering CO_2 the project provides local employment and is a valuable wildlife habitat.

Climate Care is involved in a number of other projects and is able to fund a growing number of new ones each year. In 2005 we expect to take on a liability to reduce CO_2 in the atmosphere by 100,000 tonnes.

Climate Care has a wide client base – from large corporates to SMEs and individuals. Clients tend to offset the emissions from their flying, driving or processes. Alternatively they offset emissions on behalf of their customers and stakeholders for promotional reasons.

Whether your interest is in reducing your global warming or becoming involved in sustainable development projects, Climate Care can help.

**For further details see www.climatecare.org
or contact tom.morton@climatecare.org**

Carbon offsets

Tom Morton, Climate Care

Introduction

How does your company measure up when it comes to the environment? If you are starting from scratch, then high on your list of priorities will be investigating your contribution to global warming. All businesses rely to a greater or lesser degree on energy, and in most cases this comes from fossil fuels. The by-product is carbon dioxide, the main gas responsible for global warming.

'Global warming' sounds rather benign; 'global climate disruption' is probably a better description of what is happening to our climate. We are seeing the consequences of severe weather events affecting businesses and societies closer and closer to home on a more and more frequent basis. Global warming isn't something that happens just to people in other countries; it will affect people in the United Kingdom too, not to mention the international arms of companies around the world.

It would be excellent if we could all switch to renewable energy tomorrow, thereby cutting out emissions at a stroke and putting the brakes on climate change. However, this is not going to happen. What we need to do is switch to low-carbon fuels wherever possible and reduce our emissions by using energy more efficiently. Even so, there will still be emissions that we cannot cut out, which is where carbon offsets have a role.

Carbon offsets

Carbon offsets balance out your emissions by making an emissions reduction elsewhere on your behalf. In effect, your emissions are cancelled out by the reductions, making the original activity climate neutral.

The first step in the process is to determine what your company's emissions are. This may be from its entire operation, or it may be from a particular part, such as air travel, the car fleet or energy use. This needn't be an onerous task, particularly if you have records of your travel and energy use. The energy used by these processes is converted into a carbon dioxide (CO_2) figure – normally measured in tonnes.

Carbon dioxide is a gas – so how can it weigh a tonne? This is a question that is often asked. Think of a lump of coal in your hand; it feels heavy and is made from solid carbon. If you burn it, the carbon atoms still exist; they have just spread out and combined with oxygen to form a gas. As a visual guide, CO_2 occupying the volume of a hot-air balloon would weigh about 4 tonnes.

So it's all about planting trees?

When carbon offsets are mentioned, most people think of planting trees, otherwise known as 'carbon sequestration'. This is fair enough. Most people remember from their schooldays that trees 'breathe in' CO_2 from the atmosphere, 'breathe out' the oxygen and store the carbon as wood. As trees grow, more carbon is locked up and is stored over the long term.

Trees are a great communication tool, but they are not going to save the planet from global warming. Society cannot go on taking oil and coal from underground and try to store its pollution in a thin layer of trees on the earth's surface. One problem is that trees can burn down and, if this happens, you are back where you started, with the CO_2 being returned into the atmosphere. What we need to do is look for a more permanent approach, which is to try to leave the fossil fuels in the ground.

Technology projects

This leads us on to the second type of carbon-offset project. Rather than try to soak up emissions in trees, you pay to reduce somebody else's fossil fuel use. This could be a renewable energy project that means less coal is burnt. Alternatively, it could be an energy efficiency project that means less electricity is used. Electricity is mostly generated from fossil fuels, so using it more efficiently means that CO_2 emissions are reduced.

The main aim of an offset project must be to reduce the amount of greenhouse gases in the atmosphere. However, the projects usually have other positive benefits, such as saving on energy costs, improving air quality or general development in the host community. Sequestration projects also have significant social benefits in terms of employment and ecological benefits for wildlife. All these aspects can add to the story that you are telling stakeholders.

What can I offset?

There are two main ways to go. Either you can offset the emissions from your operations or you can do an offset on behalf of your customers – because the product you are selling them emits CO_2.

Organizational offsets

Some companies are able to offset the entire CO_2 impact of their operations. This is often possible for service companies or those that don't have large energy bills. An alternative is to pick one area of operations, such as company air travel or the company car fleet.

Companies often use offsets as part of a wider package of measures. For example, at Climate Care we are currently talking to a company that spends in the order of £4 million a year on air travel. The company has a strategy to reduce its air travel by 10 per cent on both cost and environmental grounds – leaving total emissions of around 2,500 tonnes of CO_2 per annum from air travel. The company is considering offsetting these emissions through the Climate Care scheme. The cost of doing so is just 0.5 per cent of the current air travel budget.

Offsets for customers

A number of companies do a carbon offset on behalf of their customers. Once again, a good example would be that of air travel. Increasingly, companies are seeing the irony in selling holidays that are based on a pristine environment when customers have to get in an aeroplane to get there – emitting literally tonnes of CO_2 in the process. A number of travel companies now either offset these emissions from their customers' flights or give them the chance of doing it as an extra.

The Co-operative Bank has built its reputation on its ethical and environmental standards. When it re-entered the mortgage market in 2000, it wanted something that would make its mortgages stand out from the rest. Interest rates are boring; the bank wanted something else to talk to customers about, and Climate Care fitted its profile well. The Co-operative Bank now offsets 1 tonne of CO_2 emissions for each of its customers every year for the life of their mortgages. This amounts to 20 per cent of the emissions from the average household's gas and electricity. The bank can now talk to customers about the projects that it has funded around the world, as well as the more mundane subjects that surround mortgages.

High-quality offsets

Carbon offsets are voluntary; to this end, companies cannot use them to fulfil other emissions reductions liabilities. As they are voluntary, they are all about doing something extra. This is where the concept of 'additionality' comes in. It is essential that the carbon-offset projects that you are investing in are doing something new – over and above what would have happened without your investment. There is no point in paying for a CO_2 reduction that would have happened anyway. There are no hard-and-fast rules when making the judgement about additionality, but you should ask your carbon-offset provider to prove that its projects are additional.

Following on from this theme, you need to ask where the project is being done. At Climate Care we are often asked if we are doing any projects in the United Kingdom, but the answer is no. The main reason for this is that the United Kingdom has undertaken to meet targets on emissions reductions that will become legally binding when the Kyoto Protocol comes into force. If we did projects in the United Kingdom, we would be helping the government reach its targets, meaning that it would have to do less elsewhere. When we do projects in developing countries, this is not the case, as their governments do not have legally binding targets.

A final point to be aware of is the monitoring of projects. The savings are based on a counterfactual situation: what would the emissions have been without this project? So you need to be very sure that real emissions reductions are being made. This will normally involve a third-party report that the offset provider should be able to make available for each of its projects.

Conclusions

High-quality carbon offsets give companies the opportunity to repair their contribution to global warming – either from their operations or on behalf of their clients. The main benefit as far as the climate is concerned is the reduction in carbon dioxide. From the company's point of view, just 'doing the right thing' is not usually enough; there needs to be a commercial driver before funds are committed. The driver may be a need to communicate a new message with customers or simply the raising of the company's corporate social responsibility profile. Alternatively, offsets can be used as part of a wider strategy to promote climate change issues to staff within an organization.

As an issue, climate change is continuing to climb the corporate agenda. Companies must take steps to reduce the direct greenhouse gas emissions from their operations. However, there will also be emissions that cannot be cut out, and this is where high-quality carbon offsets have a role to play. Offset projects not only stimulate CO_2 reductions, but often run in parallel with the wider aims of sustainable development – giving companies a powerful story to communicate to stakeholders.

Land use: legal overview

James Samuel, Simmons & Simmons

The land use planning system in the UK dates back to 1947 and has provided the framework for determining the acceptability of development. Development may be anything from a building or installation on a greenfield site to a change of use of an existing development, or an engineering operation such as an infrastructure project. The government is currently in the process of reforming the planning system, with the aim of increasing flexibility and reducing bureaucracy. The Planning and Compulsory Purchase Act 2004 is the first step in this reform. Although it does not change the fundamental concepts underlying the system of planning permission, it does make changes to the wider development planning process. The Act includes a specific provision requiring persons who exercise functions in relation to regional spatial planning and local development documentation to exercise the function with the objective of contributing to the achievement of sustainable development. The Barker Review is due to report to the government in 2006 on further reform of land use planning, focusing on the link between planning and economic growth.

The planning system is inextricably linked with environmental issues. Strategic Environmental Assessment (SEA) is a process designed to ensure that significant environmental effects arising from proposed plans and programmes are identified, assessed, subjected to public participation, taken into account by decision makers, and monitored. SEA sets the framework for future assessment of development projects, some of which require environmental impact assessment (EIA). The EIA directive (85/33/EEC, as amended by 97/11/EC), implemented in the UK through the planning system as part of the planning application process, prescribes a procedure that must be followed for certain types of development before they are granted development consent. EIA requires that a developer compile an environmental statement (ES) describing the likely significant effects of the development on the environment and any proposed mitigation measures. The ES must be circulated to statutory consultation bodies and made available to the public for comment. Its contents, together with any comments, must be taken into account by the competent authority (eg local planning authority) before it may grant consent. EIA also applies to development where planning permission is not needed and there is specific legislation covering those situations.

Other environmental controls are implemented through the planning system. For example, directive 96/82/EC (the Seveso II Directive) on the control of major accident hazards involving dangerous substances requires member states to ensure that the objectives of preventing major accidents and limiting the consequences of such accidents are taken into account in their land use policies. These obligations have been implemented through the Planning (Hazardous Substances) Act 1990 and Regulations made under the Act, which includes the Planning (Control of Major-Accident Hazards) Regulations 1999 (the COMAH Regulations).

Land use planning also plays a major role in securing remediation of contaminated land. Local planning authorities must take account of contamination or the potential for contamination in preparing development plans setting out the policies and proposals for future land use and development within their area and in determining individual applications for planning permission. There is also a raft of non-statutory mechanisms to support the regeneration of contaminated land, for example the development of a single remediation permit, remediation tax relief and landfill tax credits.

Waste and recycling: legal overview

Jacqui O'Keeffe, Simmons & Simmons

Waste management is an area that affects most businesses and is highly legislated by laws that can be difficult to apply and interpret. Much of the UK legislation and policy is derived from European legislation and case law that have the objective of ensuring that waste does not cause harm to health or the environment. The price of waste disposal has increased significantly in recent years and can be expected to continue to do so in coming years, as efforts are made to place less reliance on landfill and increase recycling and reuse.

Deciding precisely what constitutes 'waste' has been the subject of considerable EU and national case law. It is hoped that some clarity may result from the EU's Thematic Strategy on Waste, which is under review. It is not consistent with the legal position to assume that, because something has economic value to someone else, it is not waste.

There are several types of legislative requirement in the waste sector. Some of the most notable are as follows:

- Waste permitting is currently being reviewed in an effort to make the system more workable and transparent.
- Landfill tax, payable per tonne of waste deposited for disposal in a landfill, has been in place for a decade. The government has committed to it remaining and continuing to increase.

- The UK is also in the process of implementing the requirements of the Landfill Directive. This has had serious ramifications for the use of landfill as a waste management option, as it requires the achievement of very significant reductions in the amount of biodegradable municipal waste going to landfill, forcing the waste management sector to look at other options.
- The duty of care in respect of waste, set out in the Environmental Protection Act 1990, has been very successful. It requires all those in the waste handling stream to do what is reasonable in the circumstances to ensure that waste is properly and lawfully handled.
- 'Producer responsibility' legislation requires producers of waste materials to ensure levels of recycling and/or recovery. Packaging waste and waste electrical and electronic equipment (WEEE) are good examples of this. The UK has not adopted national legislation to implement the EU legislation on WEEE, but this is anticipated in 2006. This will impact on businesses, requiring their WEEE to be recovered and recycled rather than landfilled.

Waste management

Jon Foreman, Environment Agency

The waste business's throwaway waste costs the British economy at least £3 billion a year, and that cost is going to rise over the next few years. Every business creates waste, but many businesses have demonstrated that huge savings can be made by managing it better. Good management practices are also important to make sure you keep within the law, which is changing rapidly.

The expensive waste mountain

Businesses in England and Wales produce around 70 million tonnes of industrial and commercial waste a year, two and a half times as much as people put in their domestic rubbish bins. In some cases this is literally money (or at least value) down the drain. It is certainly a terrible waste of resources. Many companies have found that they can cut the amount of wasted materials by changing production practices, and can often reuse or sell waste that they currently pay contractors to take away.

That all adds up to lower costs, even before savings on waste disposal, which are going to become more significant. Most industrial and commercial waste is buried in landfill sites, but the cost of landfill is set to rise. The landfill tax in 2006 is £21 per tonne for general waste, but looks set to rise over the coming years to £35 per tonne as a further incentive for businesses to reduce waste volumes. Under landfill regulations, wastes have to pass waste acceptance procedures, and some will need pre-treatment before it can be landfilled, again adding to disposal costs.

Legal hazards

Currently, around 5 million tonnes of hazardous waste is generated each year in England and Wales, and the Environment Agency is now controlling more rigorously the disposal of this material. The EU Landfill Directive came into effect in July 2004. It bans the previous practice of mixing hazardous and non-hazardous wastes. This has dramatically reduced the number of commercial landfill sites in the United Kingdom suitable for hazardous waste, from over 200 to less than a dozen. And these sites are not evenly distributed around the country: for example, there are none in Wales or near London.

More wastes have been classified as hazardous under recent regulations that broaden the definition to include items previously discarded routinely, such as cars, fluorescent lighting tubes, computers and batteries. New controls will also require tighter monitoring of hazardous waste producers, and the separation of hazardous materials from other wastes.

Around 30,000 manufacturers and retailers will be subject to a new regulatory regime for electrical goods, which is due to come into force in stages from 2004 to 2006. The Waste Electrical and Electronic Equipment (WEEE) Directive covers more or less anything with a plug or battery, and is likely to be incorporated into UK law soon. Its purpose is to reduce the amount of electrical equipment that is just thrown away by promoting separate collection, introducing higher treatment standards and setting recycling targets.

For many manufacturers, the greatest challenge may come from related legislation restricting the use of certain hazardous substances (RoHS) in electrical and electronic equipment. Many companies will need to redesign their components or products before the July 2006 deadline in order to meet the agreed levels for the specified substances, which include heavy metals such as lead and cadmium and certain flame-retardant chemicals.

What should business do?

Businesses need to look closely at their waste management practices and improve them to make sure they are not wasting money and to meet the new regulations. Here are some key steps.

Check compliance

Make sure you know what is expected of you in respect of waste management. All producers and 'holders' of waste are subject to a legal duty of care. Waste is essentially anything you get rid of, so even if something is going to be recycled the duty of care will still apply.

Every business should be able to answer these questions arising from this legal obligation:

■ How much waste do you produce and what kind of waste is it?
■ Is it stored safely?

- Is it transferred to an 'authorized person' (someone registered with the Environment Agency)?
- How is it managed after it leaves your premises?

Guidance on basic regulatory obligations is set out sector by sector on the NetRegs website, www.netregs.gov.uk. To find out more, refer to the Environment Agency's guide, *Getting Your Site Right* (available via the Environment Agency's general enquiry line, 08708 506 506). If you are in any doubt, seek independent advice.

Get free advice to help save money

All businesses can reduce either the amount of or the hazardous properties of the waste they produce, and recover value through recycling. The first step is to undertake a thorough waste management review. The government's Envirowise programme offers small businesses a free 'FastTrack' waste minimization audit to get you started. Envirowise also offers free and confidential advice on any environmental issues, including legislation. Its environment and energy helpline is on freephone 0800 585794, or information can be obtained via its website, www.envirowise.gov.uk.

Support your local community

Getting to grips with waste management can help enhance your image both locally and with your customers, while improving the local environment. Increasing disposal costs may lead to an increase in fly-tipping, which can become a serious problem if action is not taken. By working with local communities, businesses can help put a stop to unlawful activities and at the same time improve their local environment.

Work with your suppliers

Work with your suppliers to reduce waste and improve the recycling and reuse of materials. Working together will promote the exchange of best practice and shared solutions, so when you meet suppliers consider sharing advice and guidance on waste management and minimization. Envirowise provides specific guidance in this area.

What is the Environment Agency doing?

The Environment Agency is responsible for implementing legislation to meet environmental objectives in the most effective way, as well as helping to develop new approaches. Our work includes:

- regulating waste producers and the waste management industry to ensure compliance with waste and environmental legislation;
- influencing and working with government and other partners to develop policy and practice that promote sustainable waste management;
- working with industry to minimize the amount of waste produced by installations regulated under the Pollution Prevention and Control regime;

■ running national campaigns to work with industry to develop solutions on key waste issues such as hazardous waste, tyres, construction waste and oils;

■ tackling fly-tipping: with partners in central and local government we have set up a new fly-tipping database to record where illegal activity takes place and help target enforcement activities;

■ publishing detailed waste production information on our website to help you to benchmark your performance on waste minimization against that of similar companies.

Where to find out more

The following organizations will give you information on all aspects of waste management and its regulations:

■ *Environment Agency:* information on regulatory requirements, environmental information, tools and publications to help you to understand and meet environmental obligations: www.environment-agency.gov.uk;

■ *NetRegs:* offers small businesses clear regulatory and good-practice advice on environmental issues specific to their industry sector: www.netregs.gov.uk;

■ *Envirowise:* gives free advice and support on waste minimization techniques: www.envirowise.gov.uk;

■ *National Industrial Symbiosis Programme:* an industry-led programme that works with UK businesses from all sectors to maximize the value from resources: www. nisp.org.uk;

■ *Department of Trade and Industry:* advice and information on producer responsibility initiatives, including the WEEE and RoHS Directives: www.dti.gov. uk/sustainability/weee;

■ *Department for Environment, Food and Rural Affairs:* policy information, including details of government initiatives and consultations on waste management: www. defra.gov.uk/environment/waste/index.htm;

■ *Resource Efficiency Knowledge Transfer Network (formerly the Mini-Waste Faraday initiative):* uses knowledge transfer mechanisms to help UK industry and commerce minimize waste through innovative technologies and processes: www. resource-efficiency.org;

■ *WRAP (Waste and Resources Action Programme):* a not-for-profit company supported by government that promotes sustainable waste management by creating stable and efficient markets for recycled materials and products: www.wrap.org.uk;

■ *DTI Manufacturing Advisory Service:* provides an integrated support service to industry in cooperation with the DTI Small Business Service network of business links – includes assistance on lean manufacturing techniques: www.dti.gov.uk/ manufacturing/mas/index.htm;

■ *your local authority:* for advice on local waste management and recycling services;

■ *LetsRecycle.com:* for information on waste management and recycling services: www.letsrecycle.com/index.jsp.

Managing environmental risk

Karl Russek, ACE European Group

The notion of environmental risk and environmental issues in general involves a unique blend of disciplines, namely politics and regulatory policy, law, economics, social science and, of course, 'hard' science (toxicology, ecology, geology, etc). As a result, it is difficult to develop a precise definition of environmental risk, as it means something slightly different in the context of each discipline listed above. In a general commercial context, environmental risk issues can range from the economic impact of a property transaction derailed owing to the presence of underground tanks, to the strategic direction and global branding decisions made by a large petrochemical company in the face of climate change.

The impact of environmental and associated regulatory issues on business is essentially a late 20th-century phenomenon. Apart from a few earlier laws aimed primarily at the protection of commerce, navigation and property rights, by far the greater part of the existing worldwide framework of treaty, law and regulation can be traced from the late 1960s onward.

Prior to the era of increasing public regulation, the environmental impact of commerce was largely externalized, with the costs borne by society as a whole. These subsequent regulatory efforts can largely be attributed to the government's response to public pressure to hold commercial entities accountable for the true costs of their environmental impacts, both historical and ongoing.

The progress of this regulatory regime was certainly not without difficulty, given the need to preserve profitability and economic efficiency, whilst recognizing the limitation of available science to allocate economic values to environmental impacts and draw the necessary causal links to assign liability fairly.

In order to discuss the various aspects of environment risk, it is helpful to divide the concept into interrelated categories, starting from the 'shop floor' and projecting outward:

- operational risk;
- legacy risk;
- political risk;
- disclosure/financial reporting issues;
- business risk;
- reputation risk.

Operational risk

Operational risk is perhaps the most readily understood and quantified aspect of environmental risk, the potential that the ongoing operations of a business could result in a release of pollutants to the air, ground or water. The release itself is one variable. Equally important is whether this release will have an impact on surrounding people, properties or natural resources. It is typical for a regulator to discuss this in terms of a 'source', a 'pathway' and a 'receptor'. All three of these are important variables in determining the potential severity of a loss arising from a release. For example, a release of 100 kilograms of chlorine at a remote industrial plant could result in employee injury and temporary interruption to plant operations. The same release in a densely populated area could result in the large-scale evacuation of all retail premises, the entire commercial district and every adjacent residential property, with the resultant financial and reputational impacts.

This area of risk is perhaps the most heavily regulated, largely because it is the easiest to regulate. As a result, risk control and risk transfer are the primary risk management tools employed.

Legacy risk

An area more difficult to quantify is that of legacy risk, which will affect any company with a history pre-dating the era of environmental regulation. This risk relates to the accumulated effects of environmental impacts resulting from activities that, although perhaps perfectly permissible at the time, involved the release of pollutants or the disposal of waste and by-products. The impacts of these activities may be confined to the property itself or be extremely wide-ranging, with a visit to any historic mining area a testament to this. The concept of an affirmative duty to correct such 'sins of the past' is inconsistently applied in various legal jurisdictions, and can be extremely onerous. For example, the US 'Superfund' law imposes joint and several liability for any impacts dating from any time, however minor the contribution of the party involved. In contrast, the UK and most European jurisdictions stop well short of this.

The European picture is changing, however, with the imposition of the 2004 EU Directive on Environmental Liability. EU member states are required to develop regulations no less stringent than the directive, which assigns strict liability for pollution, including damage to 'biodiversity' (essentially natural resource damages). Though the directive itself does not assign liability retroactively, it is conceivable that member states will take matters somewhat further in developing their own regulations.

Even without an affirmative duty to clean up legacy issues, their existence can serve as a serious impediment to the efficient use of corporate resources (eg the disposal of excess production capacity). Many companies are forced to lock up idle facilities rather then sell them off for fear of what may come to light during the due diligence of a potential buyer.

Political risk

A recurring theme throughout this chapter is the risk that the rules can be changed at any time. As mentioned above, the status of current environmental regulation is the result of a tension between public responsibility and economic efficiency. Given this conflict and the various cultural and economic factors that can influence it, the level of regulation and enforcement can vary significantly, both geographically and over time. Countries with virtually identical regulatory regimes on paper can have drastically different practical approaches. Even within a specific country, the vigour (and consistency) with which these matters are approached can vary from region to region.

From a temporal standpoint, the combination of rapidly evolving science and inefficient public policy can have significant impact. For example, a new toxicology study may lead to adjusted clean-up standards for a particular compound in soil or groundwater. This could significantly increase the price or expected duration of a clean-up at an industrial site, force the reopening of sites that were thought to have been cleaned, or trigger the clean-up of sites for which no action was previously thought necessary.

Disclosure/financial reporting issues

An issue closely related to the last two topics is that of financial disclosure. The question of what environmental liabilities must be accounted for on a company's balance sheet and to what extent is relatively uncertain at this time. Developments are under way in both North America and Europe that could significantly affect reporting requirements. As discussed above, virtually any company with historic operations will have environmental legacy issues. However, it is clear that most companies do not routinely attempt to quantify the liabilities associated with each site at which they have historically been active. Instead, most firms account only for those liabilities that are actually subject to orders or settlements or have already resulted in an ongoing clean-up.

Current developments may require the inclusion of environmental clean-up under the general category of 'decommissioning costs'. Should a typical industrial firm be required to account for all of its liabilities in this regard, the sudden balance sheet impact and resulting directors' and officers' exposure could be significant.

Business risk

This is something of a 'catch-all' category for those environmental factors that could affect business output, business interruption (due to on-site spills, for example) and supply chain interruptions arising from the regulation of certain materials. This highlights how the effect of environmental incidents and regulatory change can have palpable business impacts beyond the simple cost of clean-up or third-party claims.

Environmental scenarios should be incorporated into business continuity planning and risk management analyses to avoid surprises of this type.

Reputation risk

While admittedly a difficult concept to quantify, reputation is clearly vital and is close to impossible to repair once damaged. Reputational risk can be demonstrated by a broad spectrum of circumstances, from the most simple, such as maintaining good relationships with neighbours in light of odour complaints at a facility, to the most complex, such as managing the effect on a brand of a well-publicized catastrophic incident for which the company appears at fault.

Public attitudes towards environmental issues are as complex as the issues themselves and can be easily swayed by bad science and alarmist rhetoric. In addition, the public perception of a company as a 'bad actor', whether deserved or not, can significantly affect the treatment of that company at the hands of the regulators.

Experience in managing complex environmental losses has shown that the most fruitful course of action with both the public and regulators is to be open, candid and, when appropriate, remorseful for an unfortunate incident. The absolutely worst approach is to give the impression you are being less than candid about the facts. In the absence of a full explanation the public will tend to fill in the gaps with the worst case. However, other than those groups with particularly strong beliefs or causes to support, the public can be surprisingly forgiving if they feel an incident was handled well and openly.

The role of insurance in environmental risk management

As with other areas of risk, the standard approach to managing environmental risk is first to identify those areas in an organization where there may be issues and then to develop tools to manage the risks presented. The widespread use of insurance to manage these risks has been a relatively recent phenomenon. Traditional casualty insurers have shied away from the area, given the highly specialized nature of the underlying technical issues, the pace of regulatory change and the severity of the historic loss experience relating to legacy pollution issues.

A specialized environmental insurance market did emerge from the earliest days of casualty pollution exclusions, but for many years the cover had the (often deserved) reputation of being expensive and difficult to obtain. However, the market has changed significantly in recent years, as increased loss experience and a growing ability to package the product with other lines of coverage have resulted in broader, more affordable solutions.

Another important development is the increase in risks presented to the market that do not relate to traditional 'polluting' industries. Indeed, an increasing number of commercial and real estate firms are purchasing the coverage because of the volume of properties they maintain in their portfolio and the potential for historic issues to emerge at one or more of them.

To demonstrate the breadth of value created by the application of environmental insurance, it can be discussed in the context of each of the risk categories outlined above:

∎ *Operational risk.* As described above, this is typically the most quantifiable and therefore the most readily insured. In fact, many traditional insurance programmes do offer an element of coverage for operational risks, albeit only those that occur on a sudden and accidental basis. In reality, the actual risks faced by a company can be far broader, including gradual exposures, on-site clean-up obligations and, increasingly, damage to natural resources. These additional exposures are typically addressed in environmental insurance programmes.

∎ *Legacy risk.* The area of legacy risk has been something of a success story for environmental insurance. A typical deployment of the coverage is to address the potential legacy liabilities associated with a site or group of sites, particularly when they are the subject of a disposal or other corporate transaction. Policy terms of up to 10 years have been used to replace or support the contract indemnity, which typically addressed such issues prior to the development of the insurance product. Although the cover is typically employed for liabilities associated with individual sites, environmental insurance has been used to address legacy issues in some extremely large corporate mergers and acquisitions.

∎ *Political risk.* Given the extremely unpredictable nature of political risk, the application of insurance is somewhat limited. However, coverage is available in most environmental insurance programmes for losses arising from changes in regulation, which may increase companies' environmental exposures, as described earlier.

∎ *Disclosure/financial reporting issues.* While issues of accounting and tax are outside the scope of this chapter, the availability of insurance for unknown legacy issues can be viewed as an important hedging mechanism with respect to environmental liabilities for which provisions must be made, particularly the adverse development thereof. In addition, with companies increasingly required to recognize, quantify and disclose potential liabilities of an environmental nature, the purchase of valid and collectable insurance can demonstrate that they took all reasonable steps to control their exposure. This can support corporate governance strategies and assist the directors and officers of the company in managing their own liabilities.

■ *Business risk.* Though many aspects of this risk category are too broad and complex to quantify for insurance to be applicable, business interruption losses arising out of environmental incidents are clearly insurable. Indeed, for many smaller buyers, it is the availability of this cover that brings them to the environmental insurance marketplace.

■ *Reputation risk.* The purchase of environmental insurance with reputational risk in mind demonstrates a high degree of proactivity. Such companies will enhance stakeholder perception with such an approach. In addition, some environmental insurance carriers offer access to emergency response, environmental clean-up and crisis management expertise as part of their claims services. Should a loss arise, this type of knowledge can prove invaluable in allowing the company to manage the problem efficiently and effectively, helping to mitigate the loss of reputation.

The concept of environmental risk is a complex one, which confronts organizations at many levels. Influenced as they are by both technological and societal change, many of the risk categories can still be managed and are readily insurable, whilst others are as complex and intractable as the concept of climate change. One thing risk managers can be certain of is that the degree and pace of change in this area will continue to increase, and they and their organizations would be well served in making use of the available tools to manage the risks presented.

Contributors' contact list

ACCA
2 Central Quay
89 Hyde Park Street
Glasgow G3 8BW
Tel: (0141) 534 4175
Fax: (0141) 534 4273
Contact: Rachel Jackson
E-mail: racheljackson@accaglobal.com

ACE European Group
The Ace Building
100 Leadenhall Street
London EC3A 3BP
Tel: (020) 7273 7000
Fax: (020) 7273 7852
Contact: Shaun Cooper
E-mail: shaun.cooper@ace-ina.com

AccountAbility
Unit 1A
137 Shepherdess Walk
London N1 7RQ
Tel: (020) 7549 0400
Fax: (020) 7253 7440
Contact: John Sabapathy
E-mail: sabapathy@sabapathy.net
Website: www.accountability.org.uk

Tim Ashmore
TAES Energy Management
Victoria House
Victoria Street
Taunton TA1 3FA
Tel/fax: (01823) 339111
Contact: Tim Ashmore
E-mail: tim.ashmore@taes-energy.co.uk

BRE Construction
Garston
Watford
WD25 9XX
Tel: (01923) 664815
Contact: Peter Bonfield
E-mail: bonfieldp@bre.co.uk

Charities Aid Foundation (CAF)
St Andrew's House
18–20 St Andrew Street
London EC4A 3AY
Tel: (020) 7832 3000
Fax: (020) 7832 3001
Contact: Graham Leigh
E-mail: gleigh@cafonline.org

The Chartered Institute of Purchasing and Supply (CIPS)
Easton House
Easton on the Hill
Stamford PE9 3NZ
Tel: (01780) 756777
Fax: (01780) 751610
Contact: Liz Cullen
E-mail: liz.cullen@cips.org

Climate Care
115 Magdalen Road
Oxford OX4 1RQ
Tel: (01865) 207000
Fax: (01865) 201900
Contact: Tom Morton
E-mail: tom.morton@climatecare.org

CPA Audit
Peek House
20 Eastcheap
London EC3M 1AL
Tel: (020) 7621 9010
Fax: (020) 7621 9011
Contact: Greg Pritchard
E-mail: Gregory.Pritchard@cpaaudit.co.uk

The Eden Project (Waste Neutral)
Bodelva
St Austell
Cornwall PL24 2SG
Tel: (01726) 811900/818886
Fax: (01726) 811912
Contact: Alison Vaughan
E-mail: avaughan@edenproject.com

The Environment Agency
25th Floor
Millbank Tower
21–24 Millbank
London SW1P 4XL
Tel: (020) 7863 8710
Fax: (020) 7863 8655
Contact: Vicky Quill-Bishop
E-mail: vicky.quill-bishop@environment-agency.gov.uk

The Fairtrade Foundation
Room 204
16 Baldwin's Gardens
London EC1N 7RJ
Tel: (020) 7405 5942
Fax: (020) 7405 5943
Contact: Ian Bretman
E-mail: ian.bretman@fairtrade.org.uk

Forest Stewardship Council (FSC) UK
Room 8
11–13 Great Oak Street
Llanidloes
Powys SY18 6BU
Contact: Nick Cliffe
E-mail: nick@fsc-uk.org

Manpower UK
Capital Court
Windsor Street
Uxbridge
Middlesex UB8 1AB
Tel: (01895) 295200
Fax: (01895) 205201
Contact: Ruth Hounslow
E-mail: ruth.hounslow@manpower.co.uk

The Royal Society for the Protection of Accidents (RoSPA)
RoSPA House
Edgbaston Park
353 Bristol Road
Edgbaston
Birmingham B5 7ST
Tel: (0121) 248 2000
Fax: (0121) 248 2001
Contact: Errol Taylor
E-mail: etaylor@rospa.com

Severnside Recycling
The Pines
Heol-y-Forlan
Whitchurch
Cardiff CF14 1AX
Tel: 0800 7 831 831
Contact: Tim Price
E-mail: tim.price@severnside.com

Simmons & Simmons
City Point
1 Ropemaker Street
London EC2Y 9SS
Tel: (020) 7825 4346
Fax: (020) 7628 2070
Contact: Jacqui O'Keeffe
E-mail: jacqui.okeefe@simmons-simmons.com

Thames Water Utilities Ltd
Clearwater Court
Vastern Road
Reading RG1 8DB
Tel: (0118) 373 8892
Fax: (0118) 373 8976
Contact: Keith Colquhoun
E-mail: Keith.Colquhoun@thameswater.co.uk

Transport for London
Travel Demand Management
3rd Floor Wing Over Station
55 Broadway
London SW11 0BD
Tel: (020) 222 5600
Contact: Patrick Allcorn
E-mail: patrickallcorn@tfl.gov.uk
Website: www.tfl.gov.uk

Unilever
Unilever House
Blackfriars
London EC4P 4BQ
Tel: (020) 7822 6378
Fax: (020) 7822 5919
Contact: Helen Keep
E-mail: Helen.Keep@unilever.com
Website: www.unilever.com/ourvalues/environmentandsociety

Waste Watch
56–64 Leonard Street
London EC2A 4JX
Tel: (020) 7549 0300
Fax: (020) 7549 0301
E-mail: info@wastewatch.org.uk

Index

Index of advertisers